Caring for the Older Horse

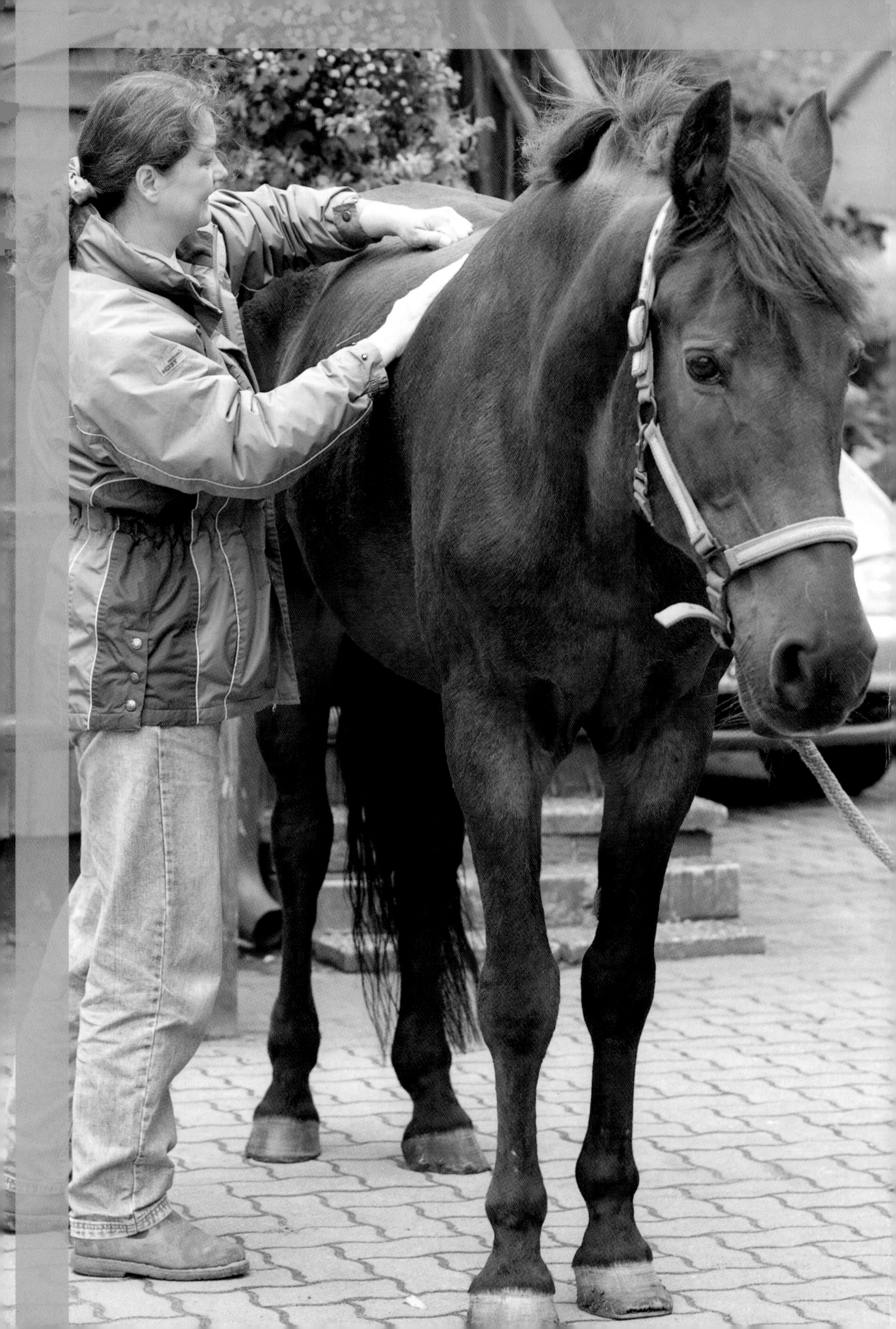

Claudia Jung

Caring for the Older Horse

How to keep your veteran fit and healthy

CADMOS

Neither the author, the publisher nor any others involved directly or indirectly in the creation of this book, can accept any liability for accidents or damage of any kind that may occur as a result of actions and/or decisions which are based on the information provided in this book.

Translated by Konstanze Allsopp
Layout: Ravenstein + Partner, Verden
Photographs: Dr Jochen Becker, Anneke Bosse, Dr Kathrin Irgang, Claudia Jung, Christiane Slawik
Title photograph: Christiane Slawik
Drawings: Julia Denmann, Maria Mähler
Editorial: Anneke Bosse, Christopher Long (English edition)
Printed by: Westermann Druck, Zwickau

British Library Cataloguing in Publication Data
A catalogue record of this book is available from the British Library.

Printed in Germany

www.cadmos.co.uk

ISBN 978-3-86127-965-5

Contents

Introduction

At the beginning of my training as an animal physiotherapist, my own horse often acted as the trial subject when I was practising massage. After I had further improved my abilities and my horse had learned to recognise the advantages of an owner who had the ability to massage, I was asked by an increasing number of horse owners if I could massage their horses as well. They remarked on the fact that my horse always looking so relaxed and, by the way, they had an older horse standing about which they didn't really know what to do with any more. But surely massage would do no harm.

That way I received my first older horses as patients. Many of these 'oldies' remained with me for many years and were provided with massages by their owners at regular intervals. Their quality of life improved considerably. I showed the owners certain exercises and they thus suddenly had something they could perform together with their horse. They enjoyed the new experience and those rare moments in time when the feeling of 'well-being' was the most important thing. I, on the other hand, was astounded time and time again by how fit most of the old horses became over time. Almost all senior horses enjoy magnetic field and thermal treatments, and massages in particular. Often an almost meditative calm is created between man/woman and horse. I left such treatment sessions with a positive feeling of well-being and looked forward to the next session.

If the trainer has the opportunity to accompany older horses over a considerable length of time, he/she also learns that each horse reacts differently to developing age-related infirmities. Some horses are perfectly capable of turning the situation to their advantage if they can no longer see or hear properly. It is, after all, difficult to ascertain how advanced such an impairment has become. Therefore the owner tends to treat an older horse with greater care. An owner who feels insecure in what to do often permits certain types of behaviour that would not have been acceptable in the past and would quite often have been punished. Many horses realise this very quickly and use this insecurity to their advantage. In many cases, the 'veteran' will only have to do a minimal amount

of work and will receive large amounts of titbits for making this small effort. The owner simply rejoices in the fact that his/her old horse is still in such good condition, and allows it to get away with all manner of misbehaviour without feeling guilty.

If you only get to know a horse in the latter period of its life, it is quite possible that you will be present at its death. Over the years, I have accompanied many older horses on their last journey. If the horse has signalled its pleasure at seeing the therapist at every massage appointment, it can be difficult to say farewell. Animal physiotherapy has its limitations here; it is possible to significantly improve the quality of life, but it is impossible to achieve immortality. What the horse owner is left with is many wonderful memories – of long hacks, joint success at shows and gymkhanas or other activities, which forged the partnership between the horse and human being.

Therefore, you should not start to neglect your equine partner when it gets older – and this is one of the reasons why this book was written. It is designed to show you ways to retain your older horse's joie de vivre for as long as possible. The reward is calmness, peace, intimacy, but also, in particular, the special strength which older horses are able to give us. I wish you and your 'veteran' a wonderful time. If you have questions or have collected positive experiences, please do not hesitate to contact me on the website www.tierphysiotherapie-berlin.de.

I would like to thank all those who have helped me transform the idea of writing a book about older horses into reality. I would particularly like to thank Dr Kathrin Irgang and Klaus Lübker, who proofread the text and provided me with their extensive expert knowledge regarding the correct feeding of horses.

Claudia Jung

August 2008

Signs of ageing

Growing old is not an illness, but rather a completely normal change of the physiological state of well-being! In the case of humans, diverse theories are put forward as to why the ageing process starts earlier in some people than in others. Scientists, for example, have identified certain genes which trigger or accelerate the ageing process.

This, however, is only one part of the process that leads to ageing in any living being. For human beings, the best way to remain fit and healthy is to have a good lifestyle with balanced nutrition and plenty of exercise. For horses, these principles are pretty much the same.

(Photo: Slawik)

When is a horse considered to be old?

Several factors play an important role in the ageing process of horses:

- genetic predisposition
- nutrition
- rearing conditions
- environmental conditions

Important deficits in, for example, the nutrition of a mare in foal, or during the first few years of the foal's life, cannot be made good in later years. The term 'environmental conditions' not only encompasses the way the horse is kept, but also its state of (lasting) stress, and whether the horse is asked to perform too much or too little, both physically and mentally.

It is therefore impossible to say, with complete certainty, when a horse is old. A year in the life of the horse equates approximately to three years in a human's: that means a 20-year-old mature horse is approximately 60 human years old. Depending on the way one looks at these things, one could maybe speak of old age here. It is, however, the case that some horses appear old even when they are still relatively young, whereas other horses still seem young even in old age. This is dependent on the above-mentioned factors.

If we approach the subject of ageing from the point of view of traditional Chinese medicine, we would first consider the three building blocks of life: Yin (essence), Qi (energy) and Shen (mind). These are so

This 30-year-old Warmblood mare certainly does not look her age.
(Photo: Jung)

precious and indispensable that they are called the 'Three Treasures' in China. They always need to be kept or brought into balance, so that the body and mind are in harmony. Yin gives structure to all organic life. It is the prerequisite or in other words the root of life. It is the energy of growth and change. Yin is divided into pre-natal and post-natal Yin. The pre-natal Yin is delivered through the parents and contains all individual growth information. It is used up and balanced through the post-natal Yin. This Yin is responsible for the endocrine system, growth and the sexual maturing process, but also for the brain. Yin gives us vitality and determines our ability to recover from any illness.

Qi is responsible for the short-term cycles, for example, for breathing and digestion. Any lack of it is signified through tiredness, exhaustion and shortness of breath. Yin and Qi form the basis for Shen. If they are strong, the power of the Shen also becomes visible. It is said that one can see the Shen of a person through their personality and through the expression of the eyes.

When the body is no longer able to produce Yin, it dies. The rhythm of Yin is the natural process of development and decline. The decline can be accelerated through adopting an incorrect way of life (nutrition, stress), or can be slowed down through a particularly careful conduct of life.

This is an extremely simplified representation of the ageing process from the viewpoint of traditional Chinese medicine. Even here, the important things are what your parents supply you with and the conditions of life that influence its consumption.

Musculature

The musculature forms the active part of the locomotive system. Amongst other things it is responsible for forward motion; it takes over a part of the burden of the body and in addition takes part in the maintenance of balance in any being.

With age, a horse's muscles grow weaker and lose mass. On the one hand, this results from a reduced mobility of older horses, on the other presumably from an age-related change of the vascular system. These changes lead to a limited supply of blood to the skeletal musculature. Using the hindquarters as an example, muscular weakness has the effect that very older horses are able to get up only with difficulty, or not at all. Older horses, therefore, often don't lie down anymore, or only when they know that a human is present to help them get up. Some older horses also develop their own system for getting up, by first 'sitting on their bum', waiting for a moment to gather enough strength, and then getting up with a swinging motion.

Not only can you see the state of the muscles, but you can also feel it. Good musculature feels powerful but also flexible. If the horse lacks musculature, the flesh feels soft and spongy; tense musculature on the other hand feels rock hard. It requires a bit of practice until you can properly assess the state of the musculature of a horse you are treating. It therefore makes sense to compare the feel of different horses in order to be able to judge the state of your own horse more competently.

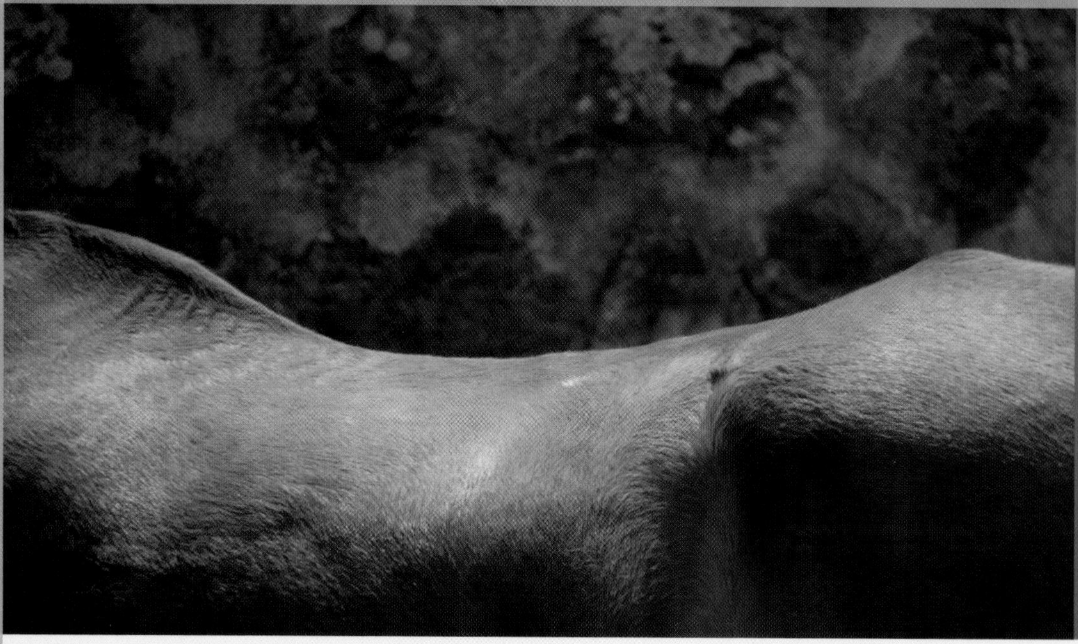

Lack of exercise leads to a deterioration of the back and abdominal muscles – a hollowed-out back is the result. (Photo: Slawik)

Recent studies in humans have revealed that regular power training slows down the decline of the muscles and improves their strength. Under the assumption that the muscles of the horse act in a similar way, training needs to be adjusted to the needs of the older horse and continued regularly.

In the event that this is not possible because of illness, the musculature goes into decline; the older horse looks gaunt and bony. In the case of a lack of movement this occurs amongst other places in the region of the back and abdomen, and leads to a hollowed-out back and a hanging abdomen.

You will recognise good back muscles through the fact that the long back muscle (longissimus dorsi) fills out the flanks well and frames the spine evenly on both sides. If the back muscles are particularly well developed, the long back muscle even rises slightly above the spine. Defective muscles are defined by a back muscle which is flat or has even sunk below the spine, and the spine is raised prominently not only in the front where the saddle lies, but also in the area of the flanks.

The muscles of the abdominal area ensure that the flanks are round and well filled. The four abdominal muscles (straight abdominal muscle, internal and external oblique abdominal muscles and the transverse abdominal muscle) form a contracting girdle, which is able to adapt itself to the weight and volume of the internal organs. Well-trained abdominal muscles under stress offer a counter pressure to the back muscles because they carry the trunk, which therefore does not hang from the spine.

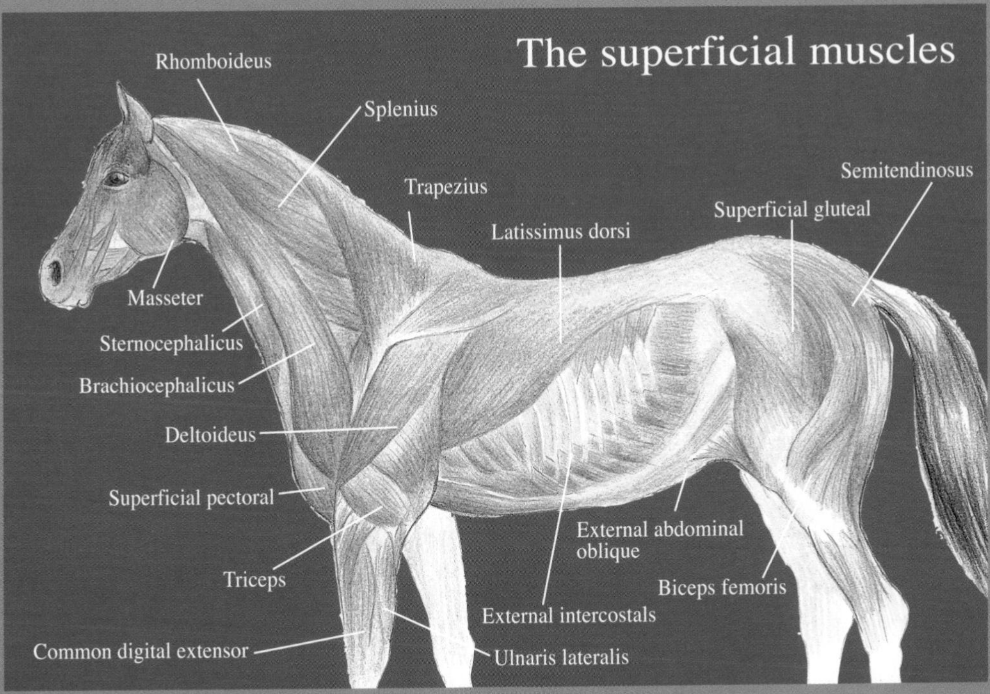

You will recognise good back muscles through the fact that the long back muscle (longissimus dorsi) fills out the flanks well and frames the thoracic spine evenly on both sides. The abdominal muscles from a contractile carrying belt, which is able to adapt itself to the weight and volume of the internal organs. (Illustrations: Denmann)

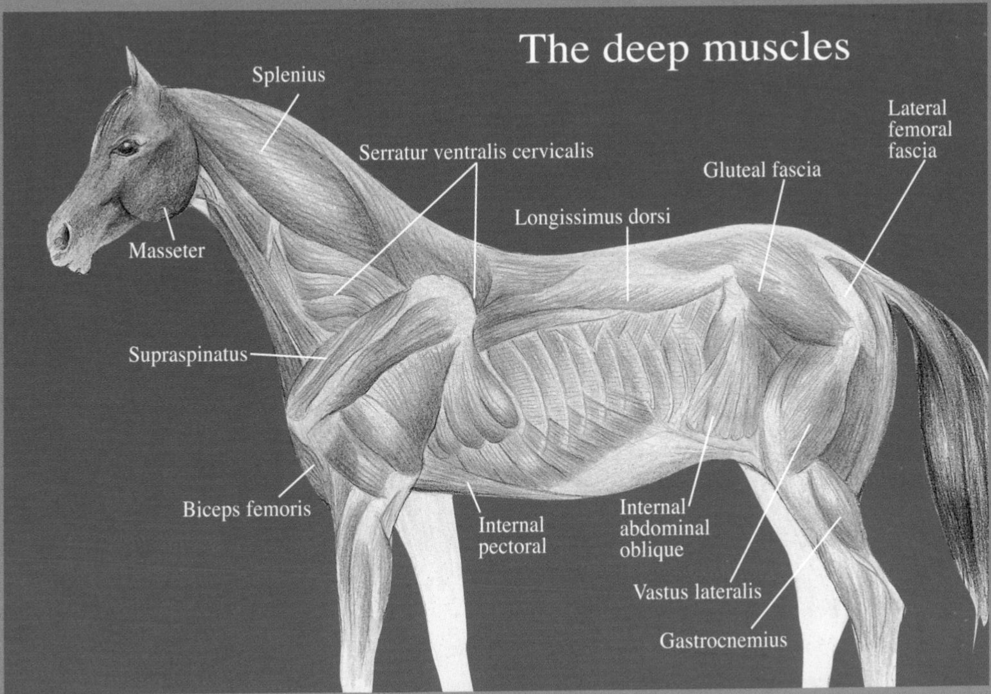

In equine circles there is a saying: 'No abdomen, no back'. Accordingly, our training and exercise programme should always have the goal of building up or maintaining the abdominal muscles. This does not only apply to older horses, by the way, but to horses of all ages. You will find practical exercises for this from page 96 onwards.

Tendons, ligaments and joints

Functional abnormalities in the tendons, ligaments and joints (here predominantly arthrosis) lead to pain and restricted mobility.

Idleness leads to stagnation:
the less older horses are exercised,
the stiffer they become.

Ligaments are found on the inside as well as the outside of the joints. Apart from providing flexibility, their task is also stabilisation. The tendons connect muscles and bones, and allow muscles to have an effect at a distance. Like the ligaments, they consist of firm connective tissue made from very fine fibres, the so-called fibrils.

Tendons, ligaments and the joints lose their elasticity in the older horse; the fibres wear out, which increases the risk of accidents due to twisting or overuse. This needs to be considered during the training and mobility programme.

What is arthrosis?

Arthrosis is a term used to describe the reduction of the cartilage tissues in the joints and calcification at their edges. The cartilage ensures that, at the mobile connection of two or more bones, these do not rub against each other. In addition, it forms a buffer, which absorbs impacts and thereby protects the ends of the bones. The synovial fluid supplies the cartilage with important nutrients. It is found in the articular capsule, which holds the joint together.

In a healthy joint, the cartilage (light blue) is smooth, is well supplied and able to absorb impacts. When the cartilage changes (on the right), the results are inflammation and pain, and later additional bone growth. The cartilage is no longer able to absorb impacts. (Drawing: Mähler)

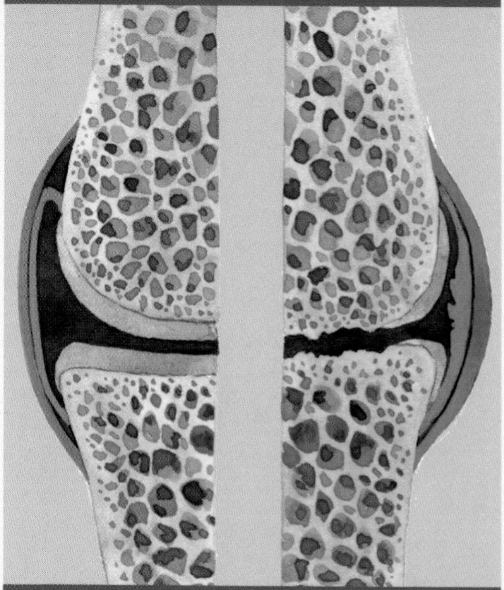

In healthy joints the cartilage ends are smooth and well supplied by the synovial fluid. In the case of arthrosis, the circulation in the joint changes through vasculitis and swelling. This leads to the synovial fluid becoming diluted, and it is no longer able to supply the cartilage sufficiently. The cartilage loses its buffer effect, which leads to friction between the bones touching each other, which in turn leads to pain, inflammation and changes in the bones (calcification for example).

In younger horses, arthrosis occurs primarily through too much stress on joints and bones and through the resulting inflammation. High levels of stress occur through:

- deformities of the skeletal system, for example, cow hocks on the hind legs, which often lead to spavins owing to the high stress placed on the inside surfaces of the hocks
- incorrect training and thereby overworking the horse when asked to perform at a high level
- overworking the horse by riding on unsuitable surfaces or through straining, twisting or spraining a joint
- not fully healed or untreated inflammation of the joints

In the case of older horses, arthrosis develops as a consequence of the facts mentioned above, through wear and tear of the affected structures, or through a repeated incorrect stress that occurs when a horse adopts a position (or, usually, has already adopted it) that saves the affected area from excessive pain. If the older horse, for example, feels pain in his right hind leg for any reason, he will attempt to relieve the stress in that area and transfer it to the diagonal, in other words the left front limb, which is now overloaded. The best-known changes that are often mentioned in combination with arthrosis are:

→ **Spavins:** This disorder describes calcification in the lower inside area of the hock. In the end stage deformities occur in the individual joints that form the complex hock joint.

→ **Ringbone:** This condition defines calcification in the area of the pasterns and their ligaments. Depending on whether the calcification occurs on the centre of the pastern or just above the coronet band, they are termed as high or low ringbone.

→ **Navicular syndrome:** The navicular bone lies on the back of the distal interphalangeal (coffin) joint. The deep digital flexor tendon passes over the back surface of the navicular bone and, interposed between it and the bone, is the navicular bursa, a small fluid filled sac which links with the coffin joint. Changes in the navicular bone occur almost exclusively in the front feet and may affect the entire navicular region including the flexor tendon. If the condition worsens, deformities develop between the tendon and the bone.

Symptoms of arthrosis

In older horses, arthroses are defined by a limited mobility of the affected joint and so-called warming-up stiffness: after a period of rest the horse needs to warm up before it moves smoothly. The paces of an older horse lack the elasticity and dynamism they used to have, the veteran looks slightly stiff all over, a state which worsens in cold and wet weather.

In the later stages, arthritic joints are defined by a distinct increase in their circumference. If the arthrosis is activated, in other words particularly painful at certain times, owing to inflammatory processes, the horse will also probably be lame.

Help for the horse afflicted with arthrosis

Arthrosis cannot be cured. Therefore it is particularly important to start treatment as soon as possible, in order to be able to slow down the course of the illness significantly. Once the arthrosis has become chronic you can help ease the pain with a number of home remedies and thus significantly improve the quality of life of the older horse.

Relief from inflammation can be achieved, for example, with poultices of Fuller's earth or low-fat quark. You can get Fuller's earth as a powder at the chemist – please observe that it is only to be used externally. The Fuller's earth is mixed with water and then applied to the

The pastern joint of the right front leg is visibly thickened and the mobility is limited – typical signs of advanced arthrosis. (Photo: Bosse)

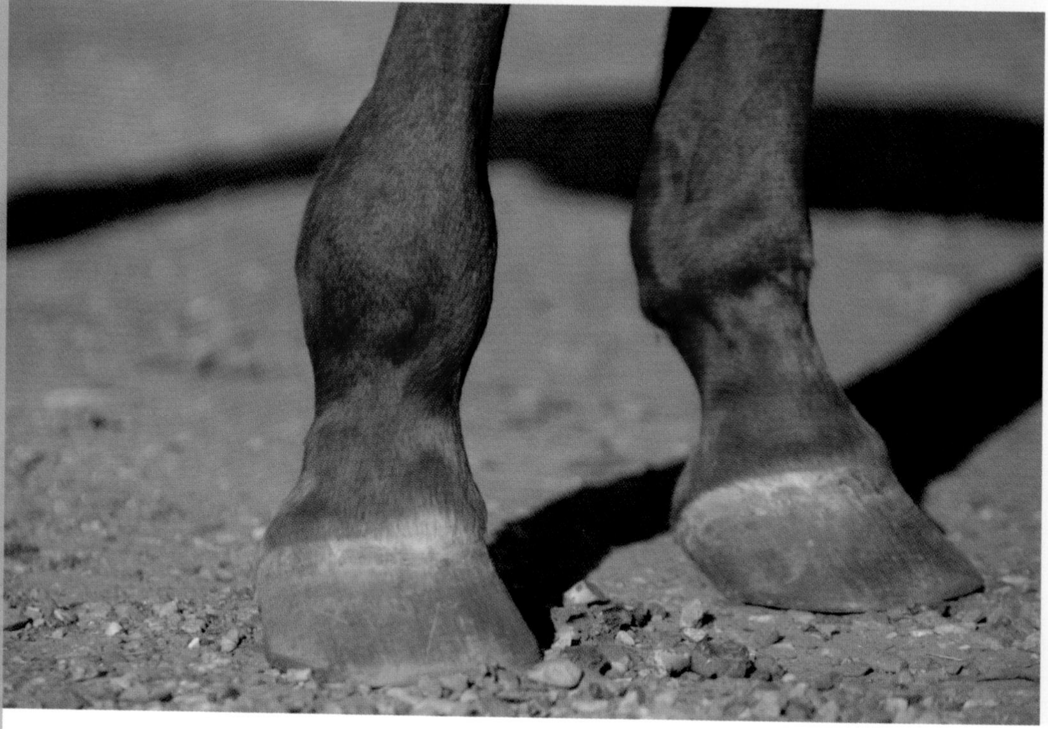

afflicted area. After it has dried out it should be brushed out thoroughly.
Quark has a pleasant working effect if it is spread on a soft piece of cloth and then pressed onto the afflicted joint. It is then held in place with a bandage firmly wrapped around it and left on for between 30 and 60 minutes to have an effect. Afterwards it is washed off the coat with water.

Holistic therapies for arthrosis

It is possible to improve the state of well-being of an older horse suffering from arthrosis with massage, thermal applications, magnetic field therapy, targeted motion therapy and, if appropirate, with herbal remedies. References concerning these can be found in the corresponding sections in this book.
Homeopathic remedies and acupuncture can also be used to ease the pain. It is of great importance that the therapist receives appropriate training in order for the treatment to be successful.
Only veterinary surgeons can treat horses with acupuncture or homeopathy in the UK.

Cardiovascular and respiratory systems

With advancing age, the efficiency of the cardiovascular and respiratory systems declines. This expresses itself through the fact that the older horse becomes short of breath and tires more easily. Strenuous activities become difficult to carry out because the organs are not supplied with sufficient oxygen. This means that the horse is no longer supplied with sufficient energy. Well-regulated exercise on the other hand gets the cardiovascular system going and the entire body is sufficiently supplied with blood and oxygen.

The aged horse is no longer able to react as quickly to extreme environmental circumstances. Older horses cannot cope very well with extreme heat, and need free access to a field shelter, or trees which supply enough shade. As they often no longer have the strength to hold their own against younger horses, enough shade must be provided for all horses, so that the younger horses do not chase the old ones away, on top of all the other stress the older horse endures. If this is not observed, severe cardiovascular problems can occur.

On the other hand, older horses have problems with cold and wet weather as well. All warm-blooded creatures, including the horse, need to maintain their body temperature at an optimum level, as all biological processes are dependent on the temperature. In this context, the thyroid

Even if the horse has never needed a rug in its life, in old age it may be sensible to keep an older horse warm with a rug when it is extremely cold. (Photo: Slawik)

gland plays an important role because it controls many of the metabolic processes in the body and in the cells and regulates energy transfer, and so it contributes considerably to the thermal regulation of the body. As the activity of the thyroid gland declines with age, the older horse requires more energy for thermal regulation in order not to feel cold. Therefore it makes sense to rug up your older horse in winter (see also page 63).

Heart problems can occur frequently in older horses. The latest research shows in particular that valvular insufficiency of the mitral valve is common. When a horse has this condition the cardiac valves on the left (mitral valves) close insufficiently: blood also flows through during the time in which the cardiac valves should in fact be closed. Currently, the options for treatment of heart conditions in older horses are both very limited and very expensive. Horses with heart conditions have a weak constitution, and they sweat more readily than healthy horses. Holistic treatment processes, such as feeding of specific herbs, massage, homeopathy and acupuncture, can – as a complementary treatment to treatment by the vet – significantly improve the overall state of health of a horse with a weak cardiovascular system.

The most frequently occurring respiratory disease in older horses is 'broken-windedness' or chronic obstructive pulmonany disease (COPD). It can be compared with asthma in humans. The most noticeable symptom in horses with COPD is a chronic cough and the so-called gullet furrow, which is formed because the horse also uses the abdominal muscles for breathing. You need to take care to keep the horse in the most dust-free environment possible. Hay should be soaked before feeding it to the horse. The highest level of hygiene during feeding as well as in general maintenance must be observed, because dust and mould can be triggers of COPD. In every case, the vet needs to be consulted. He or she will determine how much exercise the horse is still allowed to perform. In many cases, vets loan out inhalation kits that are intended to alleviate the coughing fits. Acupuncture can also bring alleviation. In this case a vet who specialises in acupuncture should be consulted. The so-called claw hands massage, described in detail on page 85, can also be used as a supportive measure.

Many owners are also familiar with the problem of swollen legs in their horse, in particular if the horse is not allowed, or is unable, to get the exercise it requires. Given that swollen legs do not as a rule cause acute problems, and there is no sufficient medical explanation, they are not classified as a disease.

Swollen legs are often caused by reduced of function of lymphatic vessels, so that the lymph cannot be carried away properly. Swollen legs in that case would represent lymphatic oedema. As the propensity for the formation of oedema increases with age, older horses more frequently have swollen legs. They require more exercise in order to achieve a reduction in the swelling than would be the case in younger horses.

Use of a special inhalation kit can significantly alleviate the breathing process in an older horse with chronic respiratory diseases and thus improve its well-being. (Photo: Bosse)

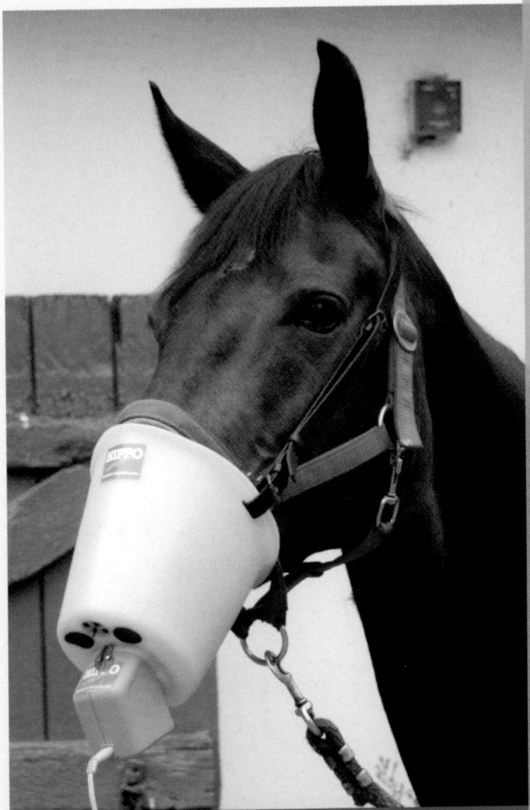

Coat and metabolism

Just as in humans, horses become 'old and grey' – the coat loses its colour, in particular in the area of the head.

It is of special significance that older horses take longer to change from their winter coat to their summer coat, and vice versa; sometimes the change of coat does not occur at all. The change of the coat is connected to the sexual cycle and bursts of activity of the thyroid gland and the adrenal glands. It is triggered by temperature changes in the different seasons and the influence of daylight, amongst other things.

Once the change of coat slows down the old winter coat stresses the cardiovascular system during the summer months. (Photo: Jung)

Old and grey – this also applies to horses. (Photo: Slawik)

Therefore, older horses often still have a thick coat right into the summer months, which is an extra load on the cardiovascular system. Good grooming and regular intensive massage (page 72ff.) or clipping can help address this problem.

The delayed change of coat, however, should not be confused with a disease that often occurs in horses and ponies, namely equine Cushing's syndrome (ECS), also called hyperadrenocorticism. This disease is caused by excessive production of hormones from the cells of the pituitary gland (hypophysis). It is thought that this excessive hormone production may often be triggered by a benign tumour in the pituitary gland. The hormones produced in the pituitary gland are transported via the bloodstream to the adrenal gland, where they accelerate production of the hormone cortisol. The cortisol helps, for example, a healthy horse to mobilise energy reserves in stress situations (via adrenaline). An overdose of cortisol, however, weakens the body's resistance. It also interferes with protein metabolism and thereby leads to muscle wasting. In addition, insulin production is curbed, leading to a rise in the blood sugar level.

Symptoms of Cushing's can include:

- long, curly, dull-looking coat, and disrupted or absent change of coat
- heavy sweating
- recurring laminitis
- increased thirst (three to four times the amount of water absorption of a healthy horse) and frequent urination
- increased appetite and take-up of feed despite which the horse becomes thin and loses condition
- formation of fatty tissue at the crest of the mane, at the withers, at the croup and above the eyes
- hollowed-out back and pendulous abdomen due to weakness of the muscles and decline of muscle tissues
- fertility disorders
- apathy and rapid fatigue
- weakened immune system
- delayed healing of lesions

If Cushing's is suspected, it is imperative to get a vet's diagnosis! The only sure way to determine this is by performing a blood test. To date, Cushing's syndrome is incurable. There are drugs available that can help treat the symptoms, but they have to be administered for the rest of the horse's life.

A horse with Cushing's may under certain circumstances have an extremely long, curly coat, and needs to be clipped frequently. (Photo: Slawik)

Eyes and ears

There is a mass of fatty tissue called the intra-orbital fat around the eyeball, the muscles of the eyeball and the optic nerve, which supplies the eyeball with a soft cushion. When hungry horses start to starve, or if they are seriously ill or are simply old, this fatty tissue is broken down, so the eyeball sinks into its socket.

The temporal muscle (m. temporalis) above the eye lies in a hollow. The Latin term 'temporalis' already indicates it – freely translated, one could speak of the 'time muscle'. In actual fact this muscle regresses with age in horses – in the same way as in human beings – so that the hollow becomes obvious. Thus, the area above the eye regresses so that the bones of the head become visibly more pronounced. This does not lead to any compromise of the functioning of the eye.

The fact that the function of the eyes and ears recedes with age does have consequences, and can lead to the horse shying more frequently. Fearfulness and a feeling of insecurity can often be associated with such impairment. If the horse used to move calmly in the indoor school or out hacking, but now sees 'pink elephants' behind every corner, the vet should investigate whether the eyes and ears are losing their capabilities owing to the horse's age. Under no circumstances should the older horse be punished for its behaviour.

The range of auditory ability, for example, diminishes so far that high tones are no longer heard. Human beings have an auditory range of between 16 and 20,000 hertz (Hz – a unit of oscillations per second). In a 50-year-old

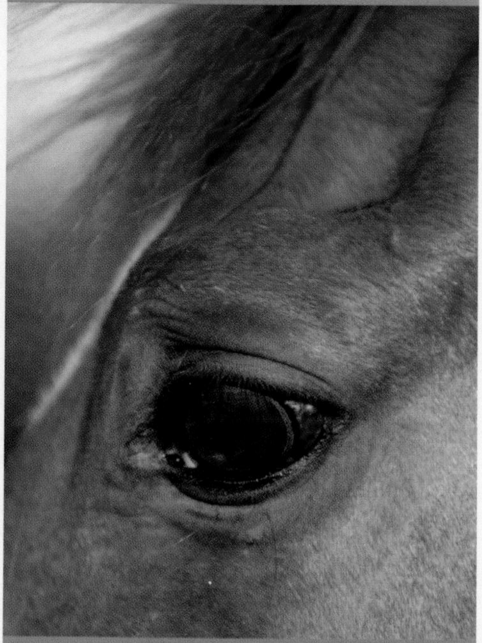

The eye of an older horse. Owing to the wasting of the temporal muscle the area above the eye sinks in and becomes hollowed-out.

In comparison to that: the eye of a young horse. (Photos: Bosse)

person, the auditory range usually only reaches as far as 12,000 Hz, in very old age only as far as 5,000 Hz. The auditory ranges of cats and dogs can reach as high as 50,000 Hz, in kittens up to 100,000 Hz. In horses the auditory range reaches approximately 38,000 Hz. One can assume that the auditory range in horses also diminishes with age, but there is no more precise research in this area.

In addition, older horses have a tendency to suffer from two ophthalmic diseases: cataracts and glaucoma. In the case of the cataract, the lens of one or both eyes becomes cloudy and opaque. Depending on the position and the degree of the cloudiness, one can assume that the visual power of the horse is diminished. At a later stage, it can distinguish between light and dark, but is unable to recognise objects. Humans see dimly, as through a fog; in some cases they see double. The adaptability of the eye to the change of vision from light to dark and vice versa is slowed down.

Causes of cataracts:

- periodic eye infections
- insufficient supply of nutrients to the lens in old age
- X-ray, infrared and ultaviolet radiation
- reaction to steroid applications
- lesions to the eye

Glaucoma is a general term for diseases of the eye whose characteristics are a damaging increase in the internal pressure of the eye.

Causes of glaucoma:

- inherited predisposition
- eye diseases occurring concurrently or previously which have led to an increase in pressure in the eye, for example after injuries, tumours, inflammation or the application of certain drugs and medication

The eyes should be inspected at least once a year in order to recognise changes at an early stage. Often homeopathic remedies can lead to an improvement of vision and eye weakness in older animals. However, eye diseases should always be treated in combination between your regular vet and the veterinary homeopath. Eye diseases cannot be cured, however they can be halted or significantly slowed down.

Teeth and hooves

The horse has six incisors (called, from the inside out, the central, middle and corner incisors) and twelve molar teeth in both the upper and the lower jaw. A gap of about a hand's width lies between the incisors and the molars on the right and the left side. In male horses, and sometimes in mares, the so-called canine tooth pushes its way out here between the age of four and five years.

The first teeth in the foal are called deciduous (milk) teeth. At the age of one, the first permanent premolars break through behind the three milk teeth. At the age of two the second permanent and at four to four-and-a-half years the third permanent molars as well as the canine teeth break through. The deciduous teeth are pushed upwards by the following permanent teeth and have been pushed out completely in a horse at the age of five. The following set of teeth is permanent, which means that the entire genetically predetermined tooth material of the horse is already embedded in the upper and lower jaw. It is pushed out of the tooth socket continuously (at an approximate rate of two millimetres per year), as the surface of the teeth is worn down through mastication of feed. In the older horse, however, the tooth material is used up at some stage, so that the teeth are worn down significantly, before they become loose and fall out. It makes sense that the feed can no longer be

The incisors of this 25-year-older horse show the sharp angle consistent with this age. One tooth has already been lost in the lower mandible – therefore its opposite tooth in the upper mandible will need to be checked and shortened at regular intervals. (Photo: Bosse)

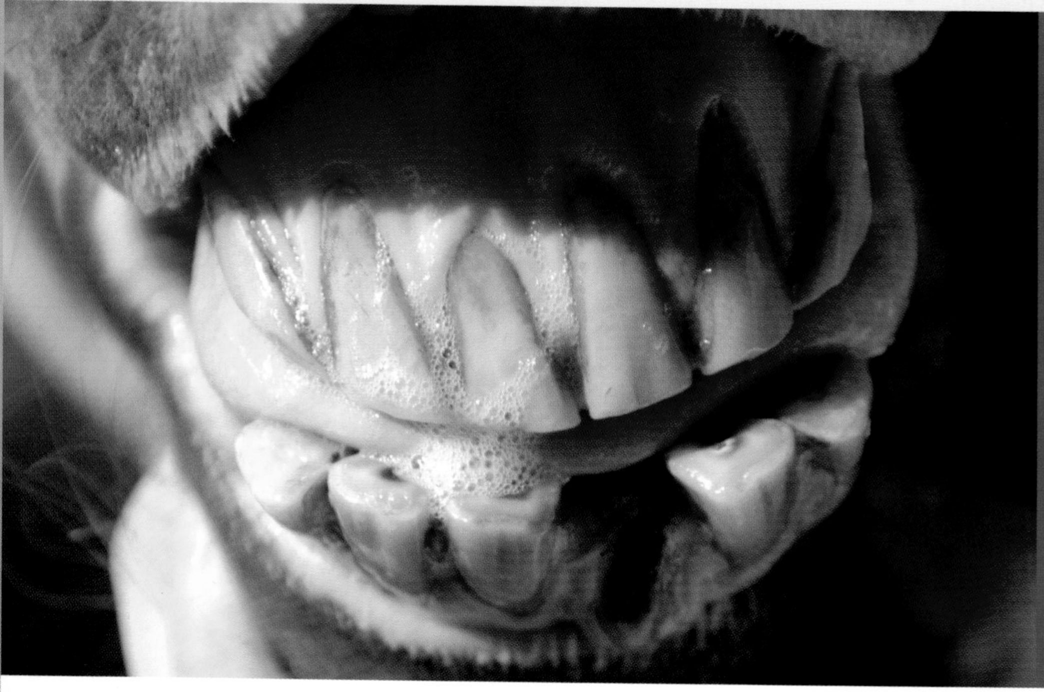

chewed thoroughly and utilised optimally. The digestion changes and the danger of colic attacks increases.

If a tooth is missing, the opposing tooth no longer has the wear that keeps it even. The tooth then grows into the gap left by the lost tooth. If this remains untreated, the tooth grows so long that it soon blocks the mobility of the jaws and can even push its way into the gums and into the jawbone of the opposite side.

The wear of the incisors can be used to help determine the age of the horse. The occlusal surface of the tooth enamel has indentations (cup and mark), which wear down over the years. The infundibulum presses into the dentin substance of the tooth to a depth of twelve millimetres in the upper jaw incisors and to a depth of about six millimetres in the lower jaw incisors.

A further way to determine the age is the change of the angle of apposition of the upper and lower incisors to each other. In the beginning, the upper and lower incisors meet in vertical apposition to each other; in older horses the angle with which the horse's incisors meet each other (the bite), becomes increasingly acute, in accordance with the course of the roots pushing upwards.

The horse's teeth should be checked regularly by a vet or an equine dentist in order to smooth sharp edges and to remove loose teeth. It depends on the horse at which interval this is carried out. Some horses only need a yearly check-up, others need to be seen every six months.

When partially chewed clumps of feed are lying around the feed trough of an older horse, the horse forms food clumps in its mouth, or

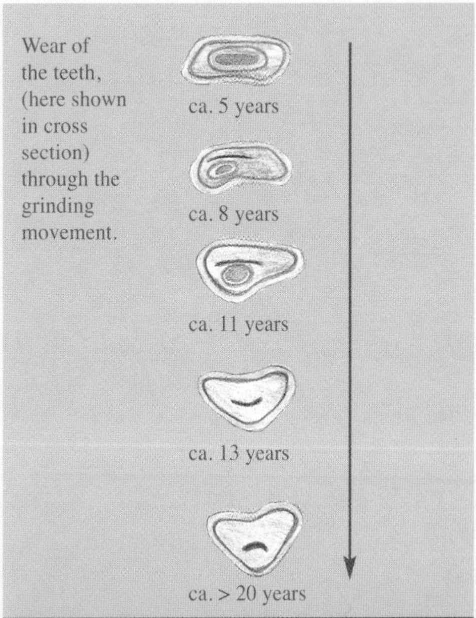

Top: The age of the horse can be estimated pretty accurately through the change in the surface pattern in the secondary dentin, the filling of the pulp cavity. (Drawing: Denmann)

Below: Clumps of partially chewed feed are a clear sign that the horse's teeth are no longer functioning properly. (Photo: Irgang)

passes faeces containing long fibres, a dental check is overdue. These signs indicate that the horse has difficulty masticating its feed. Loose teeth and sharp edges on the teeth cause pain and loss of condition in the older horse. The next chapter gives comprehensive advice on the nutrition of the older horse.

Poor quality of the hoof horn rarely has to do with the age of the horse, but is more likely to have one of the following reasons:

- genetic predisposition
- incorrect treatment of the hoof, incorrect shoeing or poor maintenance of the hooves
- poor stable hygiene
- incorrect feeding

If the older horse has had good hooves all its life, you shouldn't expect age-related problems in the horn quality. Of course, maintenance of the hooves should continue to be carried out correctly, and the changes in the utilisation of the feed should be taken into account (see page 30ff.). Illnesses and problems of metabolism change the quality of the hoof horn irrespective of the age of the horse.

Remember when treating the hooves that older horses find it more difficult to hold up their feet. They can no longer keep their balance as easily, they find it more strenuous to stand on three legs only and it may be the case that their joints hurt. In this case, the groom and the farrier need a great deal of patience and may have to place the affected leg back down on the ground a few times for a rest.

Development of tumours

Increased age also increases the risk of cancer in horses. The older horse may have been exposed to substances or factors which increase the danger of the development of malignant tumours. The probability of genetic changes in cells that are dividing increases and can lead to degenerating cells.

A large number of grey horses develop melanomas when they get older. These become a problem in particular when the growths – as seen here – lead to problems with the passing of urine and faeces. (Photo: Slawik)

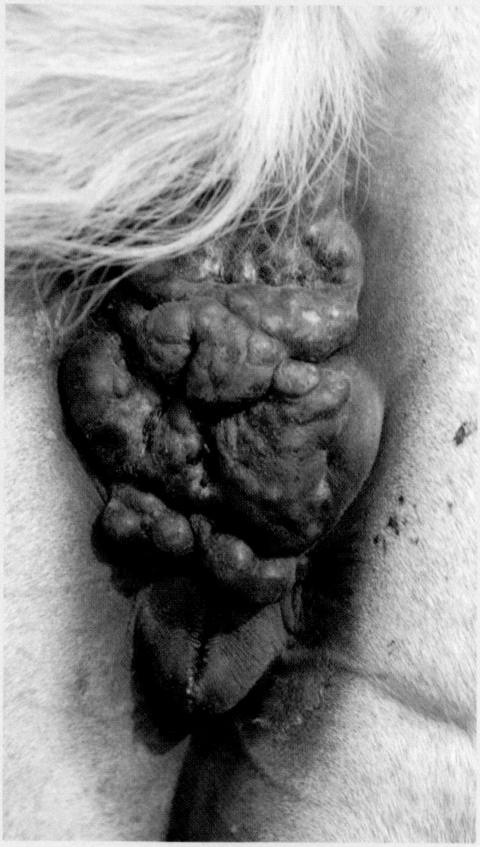

Melanomas in particular should be mentioned in this context, because they are responsible for approximately 3.8 per cent of all equine tumours, and 6 to 15 per cent of all skin tumours. Grey horses are particularly affected, with 80 per cent suffering from melanomas from the age of 15. Three clinical features of the equine melanoma are described: the majority of melanomas grow slowly over a period of many years and show no formation of metastases. The second form is the transformation of a benign tumour into a malignant tumour. The third type of melanoma comprises tumours that are malignant from the start. The primary tumour is often situated on the underside of the dock, between the anus and the genitalia. Other regions with high pigmentation, such as the lips, nostrils and eyelids, can also be affected. Malignant tumours, such as melanoma, can metastasise into regional lymph nodes and from there into the internal organs, which can cause life-threatening functional disorders. Much more frequently, however, they cause extensive excrescences, which lead to problems with passing of urine and faeces and subsequently to death. Effective drugs are still at research level and a vet needs to be called urgently.

Checklist: Show consideration for the older horse

Are the abdominal and back muscles still well formed?

The training and exercise programme should include the development or at least preservation of the abdominal and back muscles.

How elastic are tendons, ligaments and joint cartilage?

Elasticity is reduced with age – this must be taken into consideration.

Is the ability already limited through arthritic changes?

In the case of arthrosis, exercise is very important – but overwork must be avoided under all circumstances!

How well do the cardiovascular and respiratory systems still function?

older horses are less able to deal with extreme environmental conditions. Supply shade when it is hot and warmth (a rug) when it is cold.

Are the problems with the change of coat due to age or disease?

If Cushing's is suspected, it is absolutely essential to call out a vet!

Are the teeth, eyes and ears sound and without disease?

Regular veterinary check-ups help recognise changes at an early stage and a programme of counter-measures should be started.

Feeding of the older horse

There has been very little scientific research into the nutrition of older horses. The little information known is based in most cases on experience and anecdote. A basic ration, which contains all the important ingredients for maintenance requirements, is important. At the same time the saying 'The eye also feeds' must be taken into account. This means that the nutritional state of the older horse must be observed continuously, and the amount of feed adjusted accordingly.
Factors such as extreme weather conditions, stress (for example through changes in the herd, or the loss of a horse with a high-ranking position) or taking up the role of the grandmother/grandfather to foals, moving to another stable, changes in the amount of work carried out, or illness, all make it necessary to adjust the food ration.

(Photo: Slawik)

The high-maintenance senior horse

As a rule, the healthy older horse can be fed with the usual feeds. The term healthy presupposes that the teeth are in order and are able to masticate the feed properly, that the horse does not suffer from any diseases, and that it is in an excellent nutritional state (see page 40ff.). If this is not the case, special feed is necessary, which will be described later in this chapter.

Highly digestible feed, such as hay that was not cut too late in the year, should serve as a basic provision for the older horse. Cereals should, in principle, be crushed, rolled or shredded more thoroughly so that the horse can continue to eat well even if it suffers from dental problems. The state of the teeth should also be observed when feeding straw and very coarse hay. In the event that the hay is no longer masticated sufficiently and is swallowed in larger amounts, the gut can become obstructed, which will lead to even slower digestion in an older horse which is already suffering from age-related slowing down of the digestion.

Often, hay of good quality is sufficient – depending on the breed of the horse – to cover the energy requirements of an older horse that is no longer being worked. Also, it is ideal to keep the horse at grass, where, depending on the state of the grass, hay and hard feed may need to be added.

What does 'maintenance metabolism' mean?

A horse is in a state of maintenance metabolism if it is not working, lactating or growing.
In this case energy from the food given is required for:

- constant maintenance of the body mass and body temperature
- the cardiovascular system
- respiration
- food intake
- digestion
- spontaneous movements

In the event of all demands on the organism exceeding this, a certain additional volume of energy supply is necessary to ensure that the metabolism continues to work perfectly.

The change in requirements

Most older horses move less and more slowly, although there are exceptions to the rule. Some seniors move at quite a lively pace and cause their owners to grow grey at the temples to the very end, because they continue to behave like a teenager. In the past, the general rule was that the energy requirement in older horses sinks to approximately 80 per cent, as the maintenance requirement changes. More recent findings have shown that the energy requirement actually increases, by up to 20 per cent, depending on the breed, as the digestion is less efficient. Assuming that a medium-sized Warmblood (500 kg) requires 64 megajoules (MJ) of energy for maintenance metabolism, an older horse of the same weight then requires 77 MJ (20 per cent more). The following ration would fulfil the energy requirement very well:

Ration for an older horse (500 kg) for maintenance metabolism (approx. 77 MJ)

Hay or cubes (8 MJ/kg)
Daily ration: approx. 1.5 kg/100 kg body weight
= 7.5 kg x 8 MJ = 60.0 MJ

Straw (4.5 MJ/kg)
Daily ration: approx. 0.5 kg/100 kg body weight
= 2.5 kg x 4.5 MJ = 11.25 MJ

Oats* (11 MJ/kg)
Daily ration: approx. 0.2 kg/100 kg body weight
= 1.0 kg x 11 MJ = 11.0 MJ

Added energy in this ration = 82.25 MJ

* This can be replaced by mixes for older or veteran horses. This mix should contain all the minerals and supplements an older horse requires.

Dietary requirement by age (comparison)

	Horse (500 kg)	
	10 years	25 years
Digestible energy in MJ (maintenance metabolism)	approx. 64	approx. 77
Digestible rough protein (g)	317	350
Calcium (g)	25	25
Zinc (mg)	250	500
Selenium (mg)	1	2
Vitamin A (IE)	37,500	75,000
Vitamin E (mg)	500	1000

Depending on the quality of the hay and straw, minerals should be fed in addition (but note that mixed feeds should already contain the necessary minerals).

In older horses, the requirement for more energy is combined with the requirement for essential amino acids as well as many vitamins, minerals and trace elements.

Amino acids are building blocks of protein. Proteins are very important constituents of feed and are necessary for the regeneration of almost all cells of the body. The essential amino acids include amongst others lysine, methionine and tryptophan. The body is not able to produce these by itself, they need to

Most horses need nothing but meadow grass, supplemented by minerals and roughage, during the summer months. (Photo: Slawik)

be added via the feed, for example in soy extraction pellets. The minerals are divided into macro elements (phosphorous calcium, magnesium, sodium, potassium and chlorine) and trace elements (iron, copper, cobalt, zinc, manganese, iodine and selenium).

Vitamins are divided into fat soluble (vitamin A and its precursor, beta carotene; vitamins D, E and K) and water soluble (vitamins B1, B2, B6, B12, biotin, vitamin C). B-vitamins can be added to the feed in the form of yeast (the maximum amount of dry yeast for old horses is up to 50 g/100 kg body weight). Older horses should also have additional vitamin C added to their feed.

The following minerals and vitamins are especially important for older horses:

→ **Zinc** is essential for protein metabolism and responsible for the regeneration of skin and mucous membranes. A lack of zinc is indicated by disorders of the skin (eczema, hair loss) and an increased susceptibility to infections.

→ **Selenium** is vital for the maintenance of the normal muscular tissue and is closely connected with vitamin E as a stabiliser of the cell membranes. A lack of selenium can lead to changes of the skeleton and the myocardium. Symptoms include stiffness of the lumbar muscles, irregular paces and even lameness. A lack of vitamin E can lead to muscle degeneration, damage to the liver and motor disturbance.

→ **Vitamin A** is important for the build-up of bone substance and it has an effect in the outer muscle layers of the skin and mucous membranes. A lack of vitamin A leads to brittleness of the hoof horn.

→ **Vitamin C** increases the potency of the immune system; a lack will lead to an increased predisposition towards infections.

→ **Manganese** is significant for osteogenesis (formation of bone) and it is a component of many enzymes.

→ **Calcium** is important for the formation of bone and the teeth, for muscle contraction, blood clotting, and the conduction of nerve impulses. A lack of this leads to brittle bones and metabolic disorders. An oversupply (more than three times the necessary amount) can, however, encourage the formation of urinary calculi (stones), particularly in older horses.

→ **Magnesium** is also important for the formation of bones and the teeth as well as for the conduction of nerve impulses and for the muscles. A lack can be indicated through muscle cramps, nervousness and lack of appetite.

Recipe for 'healthy pensioners'

Daily ration (at least two feeds) for a Warmblood (500 kg) in an optimum nutritional state, 25 years of age, who is ridden daily approximately for one hour (35 minutes at a walk, 10 minutes rising trot, 10 minutes medium trot, 5 minutes canter)

Hay, early harvest (meadow): 8 kg
Rolled oats: 1 kg (or veteran mix – see above)
Maize flakes: 1 kg
Carrots, apples: 1 kg
Vegetable oil: 50 ml
Mineral supplements: 100 g

If the horse is fed coarse mix or cubes, the amount required of mineral supplements is reduced.

There is an interaction between many minerals and vitamins, so that too much or too little supply in one area can quite possibly have far-reaching effects on the entire metabolism.

Special calculation program for rations enable you to work out the correct feed volume and composition, taking into consideration the age, stress on the organism and other factors. Some vets and nutrition experts specialise in the calculation and evaluation of rations. The costs of such an analysis can often be recouped, if you find out that you have been feeding too much, or under certain circumstances have been buying feed which cannot be utilised by an older horse.

In order to examine the nutritional condition of a horse, a saliva test is made, which can be carried out very easily, is entirely stress-free for the horse, and cannot lead to injuries. The test gives an assessment of the antioxidative capacity, in other words the ability of the organism to break down oxygen free radicals, as well as the mineral balance of the body.

Feed and water trough hygiene

It is of extreme importance for the feeding of every horse that the feeds used are palatable to the horse and are of the highest hygienic quality. Stress caused by contamination of the feed through fungi, bacteria, poor storage of hay, as well as dust, can lead to extreme health problems even in a young horse. In the older horse this stress is even more significant, as the immune system does not function as well as it used to, the respiratory system may be impaired and the digestive tract has already slowed down.

You can get a quick impression of the quality of feed by smelling it – good feed always smells pleasant. Feed analyses provide a more precise testing ability. These are carried out in a number of establishments (for example, university institutes for animal nutrition).

Clean, fresh and chemical-free water should be supplied constantly. Regular examination of the water trough on the one hand ensures that sufficient water is always available, and on the other, helps in finding any contamination which should be removed. The bowl of a self-filling trough needs to be larger than the horse's mouth as otherwise it does not get sufficient water with every sip it takes. In accordance with current research, a self-filling trough should be able to supply a minimum of four litres of water per minute. That means that a 10-litre bucket should be filled up within two-and-a-half minutes.

When calculating the water requirement of a horse, you should allow at least 5 litres per 100 kg of body weight per day – depending on diverse factors such as weather conditions, the moisture content of the feed and the state of health of the horse.

Water is indispensable:

- for the balance of heat regulation (sweating)
- for the function of the digestive tract
- for the regulation of cell pressure
- as a dissolving agent for nutrition and active ingredients and as a means of transport (especially in the blood and in the lymphatic fluid).

A lack of water leads to:

- a decreased uptake of feed
- life-threatening dehydration of the body (even a decrease of water content in the body of ten percent leads to an acute life-threatening situation)
- a decrease in the speed with which the feed passes through the digestive tract.

Mucous membrane and skin fold tests

In order to be able to evaluate the state of the cardiovascular system quickly, it is possible to check the capillary circulation time of the mucous membranes: press the top of the index finger or the thumb on to the gum of the horse. The white spot that appears should disappear within two seconds and the gum should have regained its faintly pink colour – in that case the circulation of the small blood vessels under the skin (capillaries) is in good working order.
If there is a suspicion of a lack of fluids (dehydration), the skin fold test also gives a quick result: a fold of skin which is pulled upwards (pinched) on the neck or the shoulder must also disappear and the skin appear flat within two seconds.

Many bowls for self-filling troughs are not big enough for horses. If the horse's muzzle almost fills the bowl, it may drink too little water. (Photo: Bosse)

Much better suited are specially designed horse troughs from which horses are able to drink in large gulps. (Photo: Slawik)

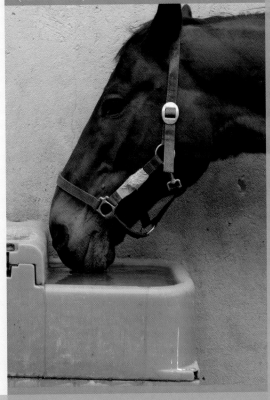

Frequency of feeding

The most important thing in the life of a horse is feeding. Horses at grass graze for more than twelve hours if they have constant access to a field. If the older horse is rather on the thin side, it can be supplied with easily digested rough feed in sufficient amounts without a problem. If a horse, on the other hand, is a good doer, you need to make sure that it does not become obese (see also page 42).

For older horses in particular, it is important to give as many small meals as possible in order not to put too much strain on the digestive system and to support the digestion as thoroughly as possible. Therefore, spreading the daily ration over three meals, if possible even more frequently, is absolutely essential.

Feeding horses with dental problems

Many older horses, which, thanks to good care and medical supervision are still reasonably fit, have problems with their teeth. The teeth fall out because the tooth material has been used up, or they need to be removed because they have been broken off or have become loose and therefore cause pain. If a tooth breaks off, pus can develop if the fracture extends into the root. In this case an equine dentist or veterinary surgeon needs to treat the horse. Irrespective of this, if a horse has no teeth, it is unable to masticate feed, in particular roughage, in such a way that it can be digested properly. In order to ensure that the maintenance requirement is attained despite this, easily digestible, chopped up feed should be given. In this case soaked cubes can play an important role. Cubes (there are cubes designed for ponies, high performance horses, older horses, etc.) consist to a large extent of pulverised hay, which is pressed into pellet shape. Always feed freshly soaked cubes, so that the mixture does not start to ferment.

Recipe: '... if chewing becomes difficult!'

Warmblood, 25 years, weight-loss caused by dental problems, weighs 450 kg, target weight 500 kg, three walks per week (30 minutes each). The energy requirement that should be supplied per day (divided into at least four meals) amounts to 89 megajoules.

- Cubes (mix with three times the amount of water, let it soak for 1 hour): 6 kg (dry weight) (soaking time may vary, depending on size of cubes)
- rolled oats or oat flakes(or preferably veteran mix): 1 kg
- Mash (prepared in accordance with the manufacturer's instructions): 1 kg
- Sugar beet (mix with four times the amount of water, leave to soak for 1 hour if shredded, otherwise 12 hours minimum): 300 g (dry weight)
- Vegetable oil: 100 ml
- Linseed (prepared in accordance with the manufacturer's instructions): 100 g
- Mineral supplements: 100 g

Cubes need to be soaked with three times the their volume of water before they are fed to the horse. (Photo: Bosse)

Recipe for cooked mash

- 500 to 1000 g bran
- 500 to 1000 g rolled oats
- 100 to 200 g linseed (boiled together or prepared in accordance with manufacturer's instructions)
- 50 g salt

Pour 3 litres of boiling hot water over all the ingredients, mix them thoroughly and leave them to soak in a covered container. Do not feed while still hot. The mash can be kept for no more than one day before going off.
Depending on the creativity and taste of the feeder, a diverse number of mashes can be prepared: with 300 g flaked maize, tea instead of water, 100 to 200 g glucose, carrots, apples, bananas, red beet, apple sauce, etc.

Feeding horses when they are ill

If the horse is ill, the feed prepared should have the following goals:

- → maintenance of the constitution
- → prevention of deterioration of the state of illness
- → support of recovery

From my own observation, older horses are usually significantly too thin or they lose weight relatively quickly. In this case the feed should be rich in energy but low in carbohydrates (less cereal in the mix: coarse mix). The animal feed industry offers pre-prepared products or feed supplements, depending on the disease, for example in the case of arthroses (due to age-related wear), in the case of Cushings (due to a metabolic disorder), in the case of respiratory problems (due to problems in the care of the horse).

In the case of older horses which are overweight, these problems overlap. The excess fat should be reduced in the long term through a careful diet in order to ease the strain on the cardiovascular system. This means that the horse is fed only the minimum permissible ration. In order to ascertain these figures, it is strongly advised to carry out a ration calculation. The vet will have to be consulted concerning the additional further treatment advice for the disease.

Special dietetics are often recommended in the case of other health problems such as, for example, propensity to diarrhoea or colic, poor liver or kidney function, laminitis, or diseases

Specially targeted feed supplements can help in the treatment of diseases – provided that they are chosen with care and not combined haphazardly. (Photo: Bosse)

of the skin or hooves. In this case, it is essential to seek advice from your vet regarding the dietary requirements for the affected horse.

If the vet prescribes strict stable rest for the older horse, the feed ration needs to be adapted, especially in the case of overweight horses. The hard feed rations need to be significantly reduced in particular in the case of propensity to diarrhoea or colic and replaced by feeds with a high fibre content. In this situation the horse should not be fed conglutinate feeds (wheat, rye, common spelt) and feeds which are difficult to digest (barley, maize). As an alternative, hot water can be poured over the cereal shortly before it is fed. A good alternative for delicate horses is long-term mash feeding. Boiled linseed is also an ideal 'probiotic feed', significantly supports the improvement of the bowel flora and protects the digestive system.

How to recognise the nutritional state

In order to ensure that older horses remain in an optimum nutritional state, regular weight check-ups are necessary. If the horse loses weight, for example, you need to react at once – this is often the first sign of a disease. Knowing your horse's current weight is also extremely important in order to calculate the dosage of medication, feeds or worming treatments. The reason is that in an organism that is no longer as resistant and is in the phase of decline – as is the case in older horses – complications can end fatally.

There are weight-measuring tapes on the market for a quick estimation of the body weight; these incorporate well-known formulas for the determination of the body weight, so you can get relatively accurate results. These measuring bands can be bought cheaply in any tack shop and they are a good investment, compared with the costs that the owner will face when the horse starts having problems with feed utilisation.

The best results are delivered by portable equine-specific weighbridges, which regularly visit many equine establishments and farms. An interval of nine months is recommended, as this means that over a period of three years the weight determination has been carried out in every season.

Some equine-specific weighbridges can, in addition, determine the body condition score (BCS) of the horse. The nutritional condition is determined by means of evaluating the externally accessible and visible fatty

In this case it is clear without an equine-specific weighbridge: this horse is underweight. (Photo: Bosse)

deposits, taking into consideration the visible muscles. In underweight horses the loss of muscle mass can be observed, in overweight horses it is the accumulation of the subcutaneous fatty tissue.

The body condition score is described by a figure of 1 to 9; the correct nutritional state lies between BSC 5 and 6. Below are the most important signs of the individual BCS values:

BCS 1: Poor

The horse is extremely emaciated, there is no palpable fatty tissue, the ribs are very prominent and the bone structure can be seen in detail. The skeleton is basically just covered by the skin.

BCS 2: Very thin

The horse is emaciated, the ribs, tailhead and the bone structure stand out, and the spinous processes (backbone) are clearly recognisable.

BCS 3: Thin

The cervical vertebrae can be felt using pressure. Very slight fat cover can be felt over the ribs. Ribs are slightly discernible, hook bone stands out.

BCS 4: Moderately thin

The horse has a negative crease along the back and the ribs can just be seen. A thin layer of fatty tissue covers the ribs, fat can be felt around the tailhead. You can see a faint outline of the ribs, the flanks are flat on both sides of the backbone (backbone does not protrude). Neck, shoulder and withers do not look obviously thin.

BCS 5: Moderate

The back is level, ribs cannot be seen but are easily felt. Fat around the tailhead feels slightly spongy. Withers look rounded and the shoulder and neck blend smoothly into the body.

BCS 6: Moderate to fleshy

There may be a slight crease down the back. Fat around the tailhead feels soft and the fat over the ribs feels spongy. There are small deposits along the withers, behind the shoulders and along the sides of the neck.

BCS 7: Fleshy

There may be a crease down the back. Individual ribs can be felt but there is noticeable fat between the ribs. Fat around the tailhead is soft. Fat is noticeable in the withers, the neck and behind the shoulders.

BCS 8: Fat

The horse has a crease down the back. Spaces between the ribs are so filled that the ribs are difficult to feel. The area along the withers is filled with fat, and fat around the tailhead feels very soft. The space behind the shoulders is filled flush with fatty tissue and some fat is deposited along the inner upper thighs.

BCS 9: Extremely fat

The crease down the back is very obvious. Fat appears in patches over the ribs and there is bulging fat around the tailhead, withers, shoulders and neck. Fat along the inner upper thighs may cause the thighs to rub together and the flank is filled in flush.

Even this evaluation can only be used as an aid and should not be accepted without question for older horses, especially in the area of the back. Owing to the decline of the muscle tissue in old age, you often get the impression that the horse is in a bad nutritional state. Many owners tend to try to increase this loss of mass by trying to feed them more. The result is that the horse, which is limited in its mobility because of age or illness, is supplied with additional energy, which it is unable to process. The risk of diseases, especially laminitis, increases.

Becoming obese – a risk!

There are scientific studies carried out on different species, which prove that over-fed animals gave the impression of being much older than other members of the same species which were fed less. The skin was slack and hanging in folds, the joints arthritic, and the general state of health significantly worse. This is often also connected with an earlier death. Scientists have thus come to the conclusion that in the event of a higher food intake, the cells need to work significantly harder and, thereby, wear down faster. Therefore, it is important to ensure even in the young horse that it does not become obese.

Horses that are too overweight not only carry a heightened risk of colic. In addition, every additional excess kilogram leads to an increased strain on the cardiovascular system, and even more so on the joints. Just at the time when the older horse is already suffering from arthritic problems, its quality of life is restricted even further. Owing to the musculature weakening with age, this means that the senior horse has to exert itself greatly in order to rise up on all four feet from its resting position. The more the horse weighs, the more strength it needs. This further increases the wear on the joints.

In order to allow the horse its feeding requirement and to make sure it is not bored, it is possible, for example, to wrap a large-meshed haynet (mesh width approximately 6 centimetres) around a round hayrack, from which the horse needs to pull out the individual hay stalks. This leads to a long-lasting, slow uptake of fodder. (In the beginning, check whether any horse tries to remove the net with its hooves and possibly becomes entangled in it.)

Another option is to string up a large haynet between two trees from which the horse also has to pull out the hay stalks individually. Here, as before, ensure that the horses feed properly and thus avoid accidents. You can also build your own hay box with bars on one side, which thus requires the horse to pull out the hay slowly. The bars must be close enough to each other that the horse can pick at the hay stalks with its mouth but is unable to stick its hooves or its head through the gaps. There should be a gap of a maximum of seven centimetres between the individual bars.

Restriction of grazing time and/or the use of a muzzle are viable alternatives.

A haynet hung over a hayrack can contribute to horses eating move slowly and they are thus kept busy over a long period while ingesting less feed at the same time. (Photo: Jung)

Loss of weight – a problem!

Older horses should ideally be slightly overweight, rather than underweight; a BCS of 6 is ideal. Once the older horse has lost an extreme amount of weight, it is difficult to feed it up again to a better nutritional state. In the event that it becomes seriously ill and can maybe only eat a small amount of feed for a number of days, it needs to have a reserve to fall back on to. However, it should strictly be only a reserve, and the horse should not be seriously overweight!

In an older horse that is losing weight the energy balance of the ration can be increased through the addition of vegetable oil. The oil amount is distributed over several meals. Once the horse has become accustomed to it, it should be given 20 to 30 millilitres per 100 kg. The amount of oil needs to be reduced if the consistency of the faeces changes (soft, mash-like faeces, film of oil on the individual droppings).

Make sure to always use cold-pressed oils. Linseed oil or sunflower oil are particularly suitable. Unclean oil can have an adverse effect and place a strain on the liver. Ask the manufacturer about the amount of vitamin E, which should be as high as possible. The ratio of omega-6 to omega-3 fatty acids is also important, and should be around 5:1. At that level the inflammation-resistant effect on the digestive system is at its highest.

When to feed more?

It is not age alone that determines the correct feed ration of a horse. There is a difference between feeding a 25-year old Arab horse, and a 25-year-old Iceland pony (or any indigenous pony of the British Isles). In addition, the work performance that the older horse can produce at that age, the maintenance conditions, and last but not least the weather have an influence on the amount of feed that needs to be provided for the senior horse.

Northern and Southern horses

Our current horse breeds can be followed back to four basic types. These basic types adapted to the differing climatic conditions and thereby developed different nutritional requirements.

In the current horse and pony breeds, these four basic types are mixed, however with one of the four basic types dominating in different regions. Everybody knows, nowadays, if you put ponies out at grass on our meadows and don't restrict their feed intake, you will soon have a 'Thelwell pony' – a massive round body on four short legs – with corresponding effects on their health.

Northern Horse: Type I – primordial pony

Initial place of origin: in the cold climate zone, humid cold rainy climate, and mountains.

Examples of current breeds: Exmoor pony (the basic type of all ponies), Shetland pony,

These two Shetland ponies are over 20 years old. As they are Northern horses they need little feed and tend to retain their weight and not lose too much, even at a very old age. (Photo: Jung)

Dartmoor pony, Iceland pony. Nutrition: horses of this type are distinguished by a strong set of teeth into old age, good feed utilisation and good-doer qualities. On our current nutritious fields they often become very overweight owing to the lush feed supply.

Northern Horse: Type II – primordial cold-blood

Initial place of origin: swampy, forest and tundra areas.

Examples of current breeds: current cold-blooded horses, Haflingers, Norikers, heavy Iceland pony, Norwegians, Welsh cobs, Friesians, French Merens horse. Nutrition: the metabolism of horses of this type does well on a diet of a voluminous feed and at times feed of very low nutrition. They are adapted to rough feed and need very little feed overall. Nutrition comprising grass, hay and mineral supplements is often sufficient.

Southern Horse: Type III – primordial Warmblood/ Roman-nosed horse

Initial place of origin: one group in areas high in vegetation, the other group in sandier areas: in exceptional cases, woodland but in extremely dry areas.

Examples of current breeds: Iberian horse, Lusitanian, Lipizzaner, Andalusian, Kladruber, and Warmbloods.

Nutrition: these horses require a larger amount of maintenance feed than the two Northern Horse basic types.

Southern Horse:
Type IV – primordial Arab horse

Initial place of origin: warm climatic zone.

Examples of current breeds: Arab, Thoroughbred, English Thoroughbred, signs can be found in almost all European Warmblood breeds.

Nutrition: owing to their incisors, which from their youth meet at a sharper angle than those of the other types, these horses require soft feed, for example cubes and mixed feeds. This makes mastication easier for these horses and their teeth are worn down at a slower rate. The molars of this type of horse wear down significantly faster, especially when they are fed a lot of roughage, than those of other horses and they therefore fall out earlier.

Exercise

If the older horse is still healthy and fit enough to be ridden, the maintenance metabolism calculation needs to include the working capacity. However, the definition of work varies significantly in the horse and in the rider: the kind of exercise that makes the rider work may not mean that the horse had to put any effort into it which uses up energy. Therefore, here are a few rough guidelines to clarify the situation.

Maintenance

The horse is kept at grass.

Light work

Work on the ground, walking exercise and approximately three to four hacks per week at a slow pace, 20 minutes of lungeing in all three paces. Slow canter stretches when out hacking, now and then small shows, trekking, eventing and driving as a hobby.

This means most so-called leisure or hobby horses never perform more than light work! And they require only 10 per cent more

Slow and leisurely hacks are classified as no more than light work and therefore normally do not require generous supplementary hard feeds. (Photo: Slawik)

energy than needed for maintenance metabolism in the non-exercised horse. They are, however, often fed much more, so that they quickly become overweight, if they are not given the necessary workout.

Medium work

Forty minutes' lungeing in all three paces with frequent changes of pace. Making the circle smaller and larger at the walk and the trot. Free jumping (without a rider). Jumping and dressage on a medium performance show level.

Heavy work

Eventing, long distance riding, driving at show level, hunter trial at a high performance level, flat racing and steeple chasing.

Recipe: 'Haflinger senior during winter at –10°C and stiff wind'

Daily ration (at least two feeds) for a Haflinger (380 kg), 25 years, good-doer, horse at rest, energy requirement
53 MJ

Hay: 6 kg
Senior mix: 500 g
Carrots: 1 kg
Mineral supplements: 80 g

The requirements listed under medium and heavy work are only listed here for the sake of completeness. Given that older horses tend not to perform them, there is no longer the necessity to supply an increased amount of feed in accordance with their performance.

Keep

The way you keep your horse has a significant influence on the required energy and thus the amount of feed required by the horse. If the older horse is stood at grass with an open shed-like stable, it moves around significantly more than in a closed stable and is subjected to frequently changing weather conditions. In addition, it may not be able to feed without being disturbed, which increases the energy requirement. If the horse is stabled, the horse is usually able to feed without disturbance, is not subjected to changing weather conditions and moves around a lot less. In this case, there is no higher energy requirement. You will find more information regarding differences in a horse's management and the effects on its well-being from page 54 onwards.

Weather conditions

As a reminder: warm-blooded creatures strive to keep their body temperature at an optimum level. This requires energy – the older the animal, the more energy it requires, because the activity of the thyroid gland, which is involved in this process, decreases.

In the case of dry cold weather without too much wind, the thermal insulation of the outer skin is relatively perfect. On the other hand

If the temperatures drop below zero, the energy requirement of the older horse increases significantly. In this case, generous amounts of hay and other roughage – possibly in the form of soaked cubes – need to be given in order to prevent any loss of weight. (Photo: Slawik)

any increase in the loss of warmth, which occurs in rainy weather and wind, needs to be compensated for. Therefore, on cold, windy and rainy days during spring and autumn, you need to take into account an increase in the energy requirement of, for example, horses kept at grass, even if the temperature remains above freezing point.

For older horses, especially, the amount of feed needs to be adapted with care to ensure that the older horse does not freeze and lose a great amount of weight due to the high loss of energy. Even if the older horse is rugged up, there is a loss of energy, which has to be taken into account. Older horses require a larger amount of energy even if the temperature sinks only slightly below zero. The energy requirement can increase by up to 40 per cent if the temperature sinks to minus 20 degrees celsius. Therefore, older horses need significantly more hay.

Herbs: nature's medicine

For many diseases, herbs can be used very effectively to supplement the treatment. However, if the horse becomes ill, the first thing to do is to call in the vet, who will give a correct diagnosis, as it would be irresponsible to attempt to treat, for example, pneumonia or an acute colic exclusively with herbs.

The therapeutic use of herbal remedies is determined through the main active ingredient of the plants, which is however significantly influenced by secondary ingredients. Only the combination of all ingredients ensures the specific effectiveness of the plant.

Horses are grass feeders – one should think that feeding herbs doesn't present any problems. Far from it! There are horses that discover the tiniest crumb of a herb in their feed and will refuse to eat it. In order not to have to give in at this point, initially mix the herbs in small amounts into the horse's favourite feed only. Bit by bit the amount can then be increased – very often the horse will become used to the taste. Supplements such as honey, mash, shredded sugar beet, apple juice or apple mash can also often help. They are mixed in with the herb/feed mixture.

Sometimes horses search for the herbs they need themselves, and eat them fresh.

Herbs in dried form can be acquired in shops that specialise in herbs, in some chemists, or via the Internet. They can be fed directly or prepared as a tea. If you want to collect the herbs yourself, take into account the season, the soil and the climate they grow in. In addition, you need to have knowledge about which part of the plant to use and whether they are protected under law – in which case they must not be collected under any circumstances. In addition, only those plants should be collected that you recognise and know for certain, in order to prevent a mix-up with poisonous plants. Plants should never be collected in fog, rain or wet weather (because of problems with the drying process/danger of mould), and care should be taken that the plant is clean. The plants should be healthy and robust. Plants that grow along roads, or in fertilised fields or dusty areas, are not suitable.

Sometimes horses know instinctively which herbs they need and nibble at them fresh from the field. (Photo: Jung)

Preparation of herbs

- **Tea infusion** (extract from a medicinal tea which is produced by pouring boiling hot water over the herbs and then letting it brew).
Suitability: delicate parts of the plants and finely crushed drugs (leaves, flower heads, seeds, bark and roots) with volatile ingredients that are sensitive to temperature (for example ethereal oils).
Dosage: 1 teaspoon per quarter litre of water; brewing time: one minute (fresh herbs) or 3 to 4 minutes (dried herbs).

- **Tea decoction** (extract from a medicinal tea which is produced by pouring boiling hot water over the herbs).
Suitability: hard and fibrous herbs (particles of wood, bark, roots), or those with ingredients that are difficult to dissolve (for example silicic acid).
Dosage: see tea infusion.

- **Poultices made from concentrated tea**
Application: a piece of cloth is soaked with the extract when it is warm to the touch and bound to the required place with a gauze bandage, normal bandage or a dry cloth, effective time 30 to 60 minutes.
Dosage: 3 to 4 teaspoons per quarter litre of water, brewing time 10 to 15 minutes.

- **Herbal poultices**
Application: crush herbs finely and fill a linen sack. Place this in boiling water for a period of approximately 5 to 10 minutes, subsequently squeeze out the water and place the poultice (not too hot) on to the area to be treated. Herbal poultices are well suited for heat therapies such as the heat roll (page 87ff.). However, they are also well suited to the treatment of abscesses.

- **Herbs as a feed supplement**
Dosage: 10 g per 100 kg body weight.
Other dosage only in coordination with the vet.

The following choice of healing herbs can only give a small insight into the variety of herbal medicines. The ideal thing is to follow the advice of a qualified vet trained in alternative therapies for animals, in order to find the correct herb and not risk side-effects, because the administration of herbs is not without dangers and should only be carried out for a short period of time. Because the herbs can often have an interaction with each other, it is not recommended to administer combinations of different herbs at the same time.

In addition, care should be taken with older horses that are still ridden at a competitive level that the selected herbs are not classed as a doping agent. This is already known in the case of rampion and ginger.

Arnica

Application: for lacerations, strains, contusions (haematomas), muscle pain, overexertion, blunt injuries (injuries caused by blows or knocks).

Effect: inhibits inflammation.

Attention: Arnica (as all medicinal herbs) may not be applied directly onto the open laceration. In the form of a herb or tincture, arnica may only be applied externally. Homeopathic preparations are recommended for internal application.

Comfrey

Application: for damage to the bones, cartilage, tendons and ligaments or connective tissue.

Effect: stimulates the growth of cells, regenerates the tissue and inhibits inflammation; slight analgesic effect (pain relief); aids in the case of tenosynovitis, sprains, over-extension.

Comfrey ointment should be included in every stable first aid kit – it aids the healing process of lacerations, inflammations and strains.

To make a poultice, take around 100 g of comfrey root and boil it up in 1 litre of water for 10 to 15 minutes. Cool it down until it is warm to touch, then soak a cloth with the liquid and attach the cloth to the required area for 30 to 60 minutes.

Nettles

Application: spring cure for the purification and strengthening of the body.

Effect: supplies the body with important minerals and vitamins, activates the entire metabolism of the body, cleanses the blood, activates the pancreas and supports the work of the digestive system (stomach and intestines), activates the kidneys (increases the formation of urine and the excretion of harmful substances), has a strengthening effect in older horses.

The nettle has proven itself helpful in the purification of the organism and has a strengthening effect. (Photo: Bosse)

Ginkgo

Application: activation of the blood circulation.

Effect: improves the flow of the blood; organs are supplied more effectively with blood and provided with oxygen and nutrients, improved cerebral circulation.

Ginseng

Application: Strengthening of the immune system.

Effect: mobilises the endogenous defence mechanisms of the body, improves the adaptation to stress situations and increased requirements, strengthens the power of resistance, and accelerates the recovery process.

Rosehip

Application: diseases of the respiratory system, state of complete fatigue.

Effect: has a supportive effect in the case of infectious diseases, increases the power of resistance.

Ginger

Application: stomach problems, ulcers, arthroses due to age or injuries.

Effect: stimulates the appetite, activates the digestion, has the reputation of having a pain and inflammation-suppressing effect.

Important: before giving ginger to the horse, a vet who is expert in traditional Chinese medicine should be called for advice. Ginger is counted as a thermogenic nutrient and could have a negative effect, for example in the case of an infected joint, because the inflammation process would be increased. Older horses without acute diseases are usually in a cold state, so many horse owners recommend the application of ginger as a remedy.

Garlic

Application: disorders of the digestive system, prevention and treatment of ageing processes of the vascular system (arteriosclerosis), general weakness and loss of performance. Well-known as a fly repellent.

Effect: antibiotic, vasodilatory and relaxing.

Added to the feed, in peeled and crushed form, the main advantage of garlic is its positive effect on the digestive system and the circulation. (Photo: Bosse)

Dandelion

Application: purification.

Effect: activates the liver and the kidneys, purifies the blood, stimulates the appetite, improves the bowel function.

Parsley

Application: strengthening of the immune system, detoxification of the organism.

Effect: strengthens the power of resistance, purifies the blood, acts as a diuretic.

Attention: do not give the used parts of the plant to mares in foal, because parsley stimulates labour.

Calendula/marigold

Application: in most cases only externally in the case of injuries due to laceration caused by ripping or bites and contusions, for wounds that are fresh or not healing properly, bruises, ulcers or burns (also in the case of sunburn).
Effect: supports the healing process of injuries, inhibition of inflammation, analgesic effect.

Bloodwort/milfoil

Application: for complaints of the digestive tract.
Effect: stimulates appetite, is antispasmodic, disinfecting, has a diuretic effect.
Bloodwort can often lead to skin allergies (field dermatitis) in sensitive humans. As horses are nowadays also becoming more and more allergic to substances, bloodwort should not be administered if there is any suspicion of an allergy.

Rampion

Application: all degenerative, inflammatory and painful diseases of the joints (arthritis, arthrosis, navicular disease, ringbone, spavins).
Effect: slight analgesic effect and inhibition of inflammation.
Please note that horses that are in pain should only carry out exercise training that is adapted to the condition of the horse on the day (see also from page 96ff.).

Hawthorn

Application: cardiac insufficiency, complaints of the cardiovascular system.
Effect: strengthens the heart, supports the cardiovascular system.

Feeding checklist

Is the older horse provided with what it requires?
After calculating the basic ration, it should be adapted to the condition of the horse. Observe all factors in this context, that lead to a change of the basal metabolism.

Is the basis in order?
The basic framework for the ration is highly digestible hay, which has been cut early, as well as grazing in the field.

Has the requirement been adapted?
The energy requirement of older horses rises by up to 20 per cent, and the requirement for essential amino acids, vitamins, minerals and trace elements also increases. If the heart muscle is affected, vitamin E, calcium and magnesium should be added to the feed.

Is the quality of the feed in order?
Feed and water need to be of the highest hygienic quality. Water needs to be supplied in sufficient amounts – now and then, the intake and output of fluids/water balance of the older horse should be tested.

Are you feeding 'with the eye' (observing the horse constantly)?
Feed and feed supplements should always be supplied in observance of the overall state of the horse – each horse is an individual, with its own rules of utilisation and digestibility of the feed as well as the feed supplements.

Keeping older horses

The owner of any animal needs to feed it according to its species and its necessities, care for it and keep it in the state it requires. In the case of feeding as well as keeping of the older horse, the main requirement is to achieve the best for the horse's well-being and its health. In order to find out which type of keep is the optimum for your own older horse, it helps to be a good observer – horses are individuals and differ from each other, and while one feels happier at grass, another may do better in a individual loose box with access to grazing.

In any case, you should start looking early for a livery yard or other stable that fits the requirements of an older horse. The horse should be moved while it is still fit. The saying 'You can't re-plant an old tree' applies equally to horses.

(Photo: Slawik)

How older horses would like to live

It is the same as with humans: older horses have different needs and requirements regarding their home. A stable that is fit for an older horse should fulfil the following requirements:

- Provision of feed three to four times daily, if possible.
- If required, regular administration of medicines.
- Sufficiently quiet feeding times.
- Other older horses, which under certain circumstances can even form a 'seniors' herd'.
- Regular health check-ups.
- Sufficient field shelters in the field and turnout paddock to protect from cold as well as the summer sun.

Horses are animals of regular habits – therefore each move to another livery yard is a stressful occasion. The horse loses the safety of its former herd companions, needs to fight for it position in the new herd, and the entire surroundings are new and, therefore, not to be trusted. Owing to that, the horse is unable to feed in peace and needs to be on guard in order to get out of the way of attacks from higher-ranking herd members. This uses up a lot of energy. Depending on the self-confidence of the horse, it requires a shorter or longer period until it becomes a member of the new herd and can get back to its regular habits.

In order to find out whether your own older horse is kept well, objective factors alone are not the only required facts. Just as important is what the horse expresses in its state and behaviour.

Does your horse go back willingly to the place where it is kept?

- Does it suffer from many bite wounds?
- Is it frightened to go back to its herd?
- Does it stand around apathetically?
- Does it suffer from excessive weight loss?
- Does it often suffer from illnesses?

Observing your horse closely for half an hour or so can be very informative – preferably in such a way that it does not notice you. This can give a mass of information regarding the rank order, the behaviour between the individual horses, feeding and drinking habits and many other matters. These observations help you to recognise the physical and mental state of the horse – and at times it is more exciting than any television programme!

If you are in any doubt that the horse is feeling comfortable, you should think of an alternative to the present accommodation. This need not immediately mean a change of yards – sometimes quite small changes that all those involved can accomplish can help solve the problem.

Most horses feel well at grass with an adequate field shelter – but if the older horse always stays away from the herd, one should, if necessary, think about a more suitable form of keep. (Photo: Slawik)

Keeping horses alone or in groups

Horses are herd animals, who live in groups and for whom social contact is essential. Behavioural problems and problems in their daily treatment occur when they are denied these contacts. There are, however, differences: some horses literally stick to each other, whilst others stand far apart in their group. This goes back, amongst other things, to the four basic types from which the horse breeds of today have evolved (see page 44).

The primordial pony (type I) always formed a large herd and wandered over long distances. Within the large herd, which offered security against predators, a large number of small family groups formed. The primordial cold-blood (type II) lived in small herds, which did not wander over any great distances. The leading mare was the primary horse in the herd, the stallion was only tolerated at the edge. Even today, there are horses of this type, especially mares, who fight bitter battles for the order of precedence. The primordial Warmblood (type III), in this case the Southern horse of the steppe, wandered individually over a great distance. It lived in a loosely formed social group because it required a large grazing area owing to the sparse vegetation, in order to ingest sufficient feed. The primordial Arab (type IV), on the other hand, lived in particularly close family groups, according to the latest research.

Depending on which behaviour type is dominant, the older horse may turn out to be a solitary individual or on the other hand needs the herd very urgently. This needs to be taken into consideration when deciding whether to keep the horse on its own or in a group.

Advantages and disadvantages of keeping a horse alone

+ The older horse can feed in peace and therefore frequently and in smaller portions.

+ The horse can stand in the cooling shadow without being pushed away or chased off by any higher-ranking horse.

+ The horse has plenty of time to gather the strength to get up. If it already suffers significantly from limitations in its movement, the older horse does not have to panic if the entire herd runs off and it cannot keep up.

– Solitary confinement is not suitable for the species as the horse is unable to enjoy the social contact it requires so badly.

– Depending on the turnout paddock, the older horse may not – under certain circumstances – get enough exercise.

– Horses in solitary confinement move less than if they are in a herd, and are often extremely bored.

Advantages and disadvantages of keeping a horse in a group

+ The older horse is constantly moving slowly and, therefore, maintains the basic musculature.

+ The horse does not have the feeling of having been abandoned, as it can still 'mix in' with the herd.

+ If there are a number of older horses in a large herd, groups of older horses may form their own herd, which are part of the larger herd.

– If the herd has young horses (fillies or colts), some older horses are readily prepared to be their 'nanny' and thereby still have an important role within the herd.

– The older horse cannot always feed in peace. If it already suffers from feed utilisation problems, it needs to be removed from the field before each feeding session and fed apart and alone.

– Under certain circumstances an older horse panics if it cannot keep up with the herd in the case of supposed danger.

– If an older horse can no longer get up without help, there may be other less amicable horses in the herd that will bully it, as it cannot fight back.

The 30-year-old bay mare and the 29-year-old chestnut gelding are standing together in a large field with approximately 50 other horses. They are close companions and don't really care what the rest of the herd is up to. (Photo: Jung)

If, for any reason, the only possible way to keep an older horse is on its own, care must be taken that other horses are in view. The human also is required to at least partially substitute for the social contact of the horse, by, for example, spending a good deal of time with the older horse every day. Maybe in future, if you are lucky, you will find another horse companion, which is equally or similarly old and impaired in its movement.

When keeping the horse in a group you need to ensure that field shelters in the field or the turnout paddock have several exits so that they do not become cul-de-sacs for animals of a lower rank in the herd. Older horses, in particular, require sufficient room to get out of the way of horses of a higher rank. In a small herd, the human needs to observe the compatibility of the animals. If you have sufficient space at hand and the group of horses consists of a large number of animals, smaller herds form within the group and pick out the suitable members themselves. Studies regarding the effects of different ways of keeping horses with regard to the exercise process and exercise activity as well as the social activity of the domesticated horse, have tended to come to the conclusion that keeping a horse in a group with sufficient space, meets the species-related requirements of horses in the best possible way.

Loose box or field shelter

Horses are flight animals that move constantly. In the wild, they wander over considerable distances in order to move from their resting places to their feeding grounds and from there to the water holes. Exclusive stabling in a loose box with no chance of grazing or having a turnout paddock is not an appropriate option for keeping any horse. In the case of older horses it is essential that they have as much light exercise as possible, so that their joints don't stiffen up.

It can be sensible, however, to put a horse in a loose box during the night so that the older horse can feed and sleep in peace. The loose box, however, should be large enough and, in an ideal situation, have a small turnout paddock, so that the older horse can decide for itself whether it wants to stay inside or go out. This way, the horse gets at least a minimum of exercise, even during the night.

In addition, care must be taken to ensure that the loose box is built in such a way that it is possible to help the older horse get to its feet with the aid of suitable machinery (for example, an electronic chain pull), if it is unable to get up by itself after a night's rest. The loose box should be constructed so that the horse is able to see and sniff at its companions in the adjacent stables.

Horses who are stabled next to each other should be as amenable as possible to each other so that they do not kick at the stable walls and thereby damage their joints.

A field shelter offers the advantage that the older horse can move about at leisure and has sufficient social contacts. The group of horses should be selected in such a way that its members harmonise with one another. Enough space needs to be present so that the horses can move out of each other's way and can seek shelter if the weather conditions require this. The disadvantage is that an older horse may under

A small loose box in the field shelter can be useful in order to separate the older horse during feeding time, for example, so that the others leave it alone during that time. (Photo: Jung)

some circumstances not get enough peace to be able to feed properly. In this case, however, there are possible solutions. A small loose box can be built within the shelter, which can be closed off and allows the older horse to feed in peace at night and still remain a member of the herd. In the morning it can be let out to join its group members.

Owners of horses who keep their animals exclusively at grass in the field often object and maintain that their horse is not used to a stable at all. Well, I know a 30-year-old Warmblood mare, who was just like that. In the winter she runs in the field with a field shelter with five other, far younger, horses. The younger horses are fed a small amount of hay so that they won't become obese. In the past, this was insufficient for the old mare and she lost quite a bit of weight. Now the field shelter is divided during the winter leaving a loose box to keep her in separately at night. When she was led into the loose box for the first time, it took a lot of persuasion to get her inside. She was incensed that she was being locked up. However, she soon learned that she could eat her hay in peace in the loose box and that no one could chase her away. Nowadays she stands in front of the loose box at feeding time and demands to be let inside!

Livery yard or retirement home

Whether the older horse is kept at a livery yard or taken to an animal shelter for old and neglected horses, the criteria mentioned above for keeping older horses should always be fulfilled. It is obvious that any type of keep that is arranged for the older horse is going to cost money. Stable owners would also like to be able to live off the services and work they offer. Therefore, a good shelter home for older horses will not be essentially cheaper than a livery yard in the medium price range.

The question is: am I willing to reduce my own demands and take on the work needed to keep my older horse in a suitable condition? A livery yard nearby offers the opportunity to continue exercising the older horse with a reduced performance requirement – whether it be through light work under the saddle, work on the ground or other types of activities. Maybe you could find somebody who likes to spend his/her time with an old, experienced horse and thus help to satisfy the requirements of the veteran. In this case, the horse owner still has time to satisfy his performance-orientated ambitions with another younger horse.

The owner of any horse shelter for old and neglected horses should agree that the horse owner can visit his/her horse at any time without giving notice, to check if everything is in order. If this is not the case, the horse owner should be suspicious. (Photo: Slawik)

If you should choose the horse shelter, the following must be observed in addition to the above-mentioned criteria:

- How are the other animals kept at this horse shelter?
- Do they look satisfied and healthy?
- Are you allowed to visit your horse at any time without prior notice?
- Do the fields and paddocks look well-kept and not overgrazed?
- What do the shelter owners feed, and what is the quality of the feed?
- How do the water troughs look and is there sufficient water supply?
- Does the horse owner decide which vet/alternative therapist and which farrier/blacksmith treats the horses?

In any case, the horse owner should look in without giving advance notice to see if everything is in order to ensure that the older horse lives out it last years in an environment that is suitable for its age and for horses in general. It makes sense to have an expert formulate a protection contract.

Most horse shelters treat the horses very well and they can live out their final years in peace. However, it remains the task of the horse owner to separate the good from the bad. The least an older horse can expect from the owner whom it has served for many years is a pleasant and comfortable old age.

What to look for in stable management?

The owner of a livery yard who does not just want to 'rake in the money' but who knows a lot about horses and cherishes his/her four-legged customers and observes them well is worth his/her weight in gold. Creativity when it comes to solving problems is also an advantage. Often it takes only small changes to achieve great improvements. This concerns, for example, the order in which groups of horses are put together – a good stable owner recognises which horses fit together and finds the right place for each horse stabled with him/her.

Rugs

Because their cardiovascular system does not regulate their body temperature as well as it used to, older horses feel the cold sooner. Therefore, rugging up an older horse with a water-resistant rug in cold and rainy weather does not fall under the term 'pampering'. It is important that the rug is really rainproof, because a wet rug has the effect of a refrigerator. Anybody who goes for a swim and does not change out of their bathing costume, but lets it dry on the skin, knows what I mean. Even if the bathing costume is dry, the skin underneath remains cold and soon cools down the bladder. It is recommended to check every now and then that the rug is still waterproof.

If the horse suffers from arthritic joints, heat therapy can help, for example the application of a hot roll (see page 87). If the arthritic joints hurt during the cold weather, the back also contracts. In this case it also makes sense to rug up the horse, in order to relax the back muscles through the heat created by the rug and body temperature.

However, as soon as the sun comes out and produces enough warmth, the rug should be removed in order to ensure that no problems occur with the cardiovascular system. If the weather is changeable, it may be necessary to rug up the horse and then remove the rug again quite frequently. In this case, the horse owner should come to an agreement with the livery yard owner and the yard personnel or other horse owners who have their horses at the same stable who he/she can rely on.

Administration of medication

Many medicines, health-supporting herbs or homeopathic remedies need to be administered two to three times a day. In this case, you need to be able to rely on the stable personnel, but you can make the job easier by filling up a syringe with the necessary fluid remedy, close the syringe with its cover and put it in an accessible place (for the personnel, NOT the horse). If a horse does not take medication easily, frequent practice helps.

Homeopathic globules or tablets can be counted and placed in suitable containers. This way, it is easy for the stable personnel to administer the remedy quickly and without complications. Herbs should also be divided into the correct portions so that they only need to be spread over the feed.

Vaccinations and worming

The subject of vaccinations and worming has caused many controversial discussions between vets and alternative therapists. As a general rule, a horse should be vaccinated and wormed regularly even when it gets old. Vets have reported that older horses can cope with these stresses without any problems. Vaccination against tetanus, in particular, should be carried out regularly at any age. Worming is just as important, as worms weaken the old horse's system even further. However, do not administer the vaccine or wormer during certain weather conditions if the old horse has problems with its cardiovascular system during this period, but instead wait until the cardiovascular system is fit again.

Recognition and prevention of stress

We all know stress from our own experience. In most cases it has a negative effect – however there also exists positive and certainly necessary stress, which enables the body to perform better. Stress is a reaction of the body, mind and soul to an internal or external threat – this can be triggered by cold as well as a chemical drug, but just as much by emotions and psychological pressure. Each organism develops its own individual strategies to cope with stress. That means that two horses which have the same experience don't necessarily react to it in the same way. Positive stress supports the health, adaptability and functional capacity of the older horse. Much more common, however, is negative stress, which may last a long time and thereby damage the organism.

If a horse does not get enough feed – for example because the other members of the herd chase it away from the feeding places – the body reacts with stress, which can lead, amongst other things, to a significant loss of weight. (Photo: Slawik)

Too little stress, in other words too few demands, however, is also damaging. This means that the training plan needs to be adapted to the abilities and performance limitations of the older horse.

Triggers for negative stress, which leads to diseases and malfunctions in older horses are, for example:

→ Loss of sight and hearing

If they lose their sight or hearing, older horses become more frightened and are more sensitive to changes in their environment. Physical disabilities and pain make it difficult to interact with the other horses, and the older horse drops in the hierarchy of the herd. The older horse should if possible be spared frequent changes of livery yards and/or changes of herd, as well as other frequent changes in its environment.

→ Withdrawal of important basic requirements

If the herd prevents its older horses from getting to the hay, does not allow them to take their hard feed in peace, or obstructs them when they are drinking, the older horses' basic requirements are impaired. Feed supplies the organism with the necessary energy for all metabolic functions. If the old horse cannot feed in peace and get as much as it needs, the horse is going to die.

Sleep is another basic requirement. It supports regeneration and recovery. Horses are only able to doze when they are standing up or lying down on their abdomen. Refreshing deep sleep is only possible when the horse lies flat on its side. Older horses often no longer lie down, because it is difficult or painful for them to get back to their feet. Lack of sleep leads to impairment of the immune system and the cardiovascular system and can lead to the horse falling asleep on its feet and sinking to its knees.

Another factor that withdraws a basic requirement is the lack of movement an older horse suffers due to illness. The horse is an animal of flight and is used to constant movement. Its entire organism is adjusted to this. In the case of lack of movement, a number of diverse bodily functions are no longer activated such as, for example, the cardiovascular system and the metabolic processes. The cells are insufficiently supplied with oxygen and minerals.

→ Over- and under-taxing, reprimand or punishment

Every owner of an older horse should ask himself/herself what the older horse is still able to perform physically and mentally. Refusing to work can often be traced back to physical or mental problems. The horse is unable to recognise objects properly, miscalculates the height of a fence, and is unable to perform one or several dressage movements owing to an impairment of movement. If the horse is punished in these situations, it will suffer from negative stress.

→ Isolation

Isolation is the keeping of a horse or other creature without any contact with the outside world, comparable with keeping horses tied up in stalls.

→ Psychological stress

Conflicts with members of the herd, fright and insecurity due to change of yard or herd, as well as other people it has frequent contact with, can lead to stress in the older horse. The owner of the horse can also cause psychological stress to his/her older horse, namely every time he/she is under stress himself/herself.

If we get angry, for example owing to trouble with our employer, our partner, the children or other people, we react with the same symptoms as described below for the horse. The horse registers these changes and naturally reacts with stress of its own. Do you remain calm and composed if your manager storms through the office in a nervous rage?

Older horses also suffer stress if you handle and look after them under time pressure. If the livery yard and your home are far apart and if you catch the rush hour on the way to your horse, it is natural to arrive at the yard in a bad mood. We then put a head collar on in this mood and lead the horse away from its friends. If the older horse is slow in this situation, it is almost predictable that you will argue with each other. Afterwards, both horse and owner will be stressed out.

It is important for your own well-being as well as that of the horse that you are conscious of these stress factors, and to learn a method to rid yourself of any stressful feelings and handle your horse in a relaxed manner.

→ Pain

Pain also causes stress. Every individual has a different experience of pain. In every case, however, it is an unpleasant experience of the senses or feelings, and because the horse cannot tell us directly where it is hurting, we need to make use of our powers of observation.

In horses, pain often leads to impaired physical expression – with the result that they are no longer able to use their body language as well as before, and often become insecure. This explains why horses that are in pain avoid, amongst other things, contact with other horses in the field. Lessening of the pain supports the mobility of the horse and thereby the reintegration into the herd.

Chronic pain can also lead to changes in the nervous system, which present themselves through disorders of the metabolism and a weakening of the immune system.

Stressed horses show the following symptoms:

- → perspiration
- → increased heart rate
- → increased respiration rate
- → shivering
- → state of agitation or restlessness
- → extreme tension of the muscles
- → weight loss
- → anxiety
- → increased susceptibility to diseases
- → increase of the skin conductance values.

Each owner of an older horse should check at regular intervals if his/her horse still feels well in its current type of keep. (Photo: Slawik)

In this context negative stress has damaging effects on the:

- cardiovascular system
- hormone system
- nervous system
- metabolic system
- reproductive system
- digestive system
- immune system.

In order to determine the stress level, measurement of the heart rate can provide helpful results. If you know the resting pulse rate of your horse, it is quite simple to determine, with the aid of a stethoscope, the condition of a horse in a certain situation. This is not only true for older horses but in particular for horses in training. Research has shown, for example, that the resting pulse of a horse is more than 30 beats per minute higher than normal if the rider himself/herself is under stress when mounted. If you realise that the older horse is not feeling very well at the moment, make sure to have a positive attitude yourself. This is easier said than done, but practice makes perfect, because the human lack of time is our own, number one self-induced stress factor, which we transfer to the horse in a matter of minutes.

Maintenance checklist

- Does the horse look healthy and satisfied in its current livery yard?
- Is it possible to improve, if necessary, the quality of life of the older horse with small changes in stable management?
- Are there any signs of long-lasting stress, which therefore have a damaging effect on the animal?
- What wishes and requirements does the owner have? Is he/she prepared to change his/her lifestyle and adapt to the requirements of his/her older horse? Are there any alternatives?

A livery yard suitable for older horses should fulfil the following criteria:

- Is it possible to feed the older horse three to four times per day, if necessary?
- Is the medication that has been prepared by the owner in advance administered reliably by the livery yard personnel?
- Can the older horse feed in peace?
- Are there other older horses at the yard which could, under certain circumstances, form a 'senior herd'?
- Is the state of health of the horses checked regularly?
- Does the yard have sufficient field shelters to protect the horses from cold and rain as well as from strong sunlight?
- Is it possible to rug up the older horse with a waterproof rug when it is raining?

Retirement homes and rescue shelters for older horses should guarantee the following additional criteria:

- Are all animals at the home well kept and do they give the impression of being healthy and satisfied?
- Are the owners allowed to visit their horses at any time without giving prior notice?
- Do the fields, turn-out paddocks and stables look well cared for?
- Is the quality of the feed and drinking water of the highest standard?
- Does the owner of the horse determine which vet/non-medical practitioner and which farrier/blacksmith treats the horse?
- Is the older horse able to cope well with the chosen type of keep?

Wellness programmes for older horses

According to the definition of the World Health Organization, health is 'a state of complete physical, mental and social well-being and not merely the absence of disease or infirmity'. Therefore you should take care of a horse's health at all times – not just at the first sign of disease or infirmity!

Feeding and keeping horses according to their species' requirements, as well as carrying out a performance and learning ability adapted training programme, helps keep them healthy and fit into old age. However, the older horse in particular benefits additionally from a number of activities. Owing to my work as an animal physiotherapist I know how older horses enjoy touch therapy and gentle massage. Therefore, I would like to introduce a few hand massage movements and techniques, which every owner can practise on his/her horse alone without causing any significant harm.

In addition: if you are able to learn to 'see with the hands', you will have yet another method available to help recognise any problems your horse develops at an early stage.

(Photo: Becker)

Massage for body and soul

Targeted hand manipulation and massage are not only very pleasant for the older horse, but can also help reveal small injuries of the musculature, tendons and ligaments at an early stage and prevent worse consequences. Naturally it is not enough to touch a horse just once in order to know where the problems are situated.

'Seeing with the hands' means that you constantly palpate the different parts of the body and recognise where something feels uncommonly soft, hard, warm or cold. A comparison with other horses can help educate your own ability to feel. In time, you will develop an intimate picture through the hands and you will be able to feel any changes immediately.

Anybody who learns to see with their hands will be able to do a lot of good to his/her horse and can feel any problems in the horse's body at an early stage. (Photo: Becker)

Preliminary Exercise 1:
Learning to see with one's hands

Ask a person who is willing to help to lay a hair between the first two pages of a blank notepad without you seeing where the hair is placed. Now move your index finger over the topmost page and try to feel the hair. With time, your feeling will become increasingly sensitive and you will be able to feel the hair under an increasing number of pages. Therapists with long years of experience are able to feel a thin hair under eight pages. If you want to massage your veteran yourself, it suffices if you can feel the hair underneath one page.

The healing power of hand massage manipulation is tremendous! There are millions of sensors in the skin of a mammal, which turn it into a tactile sheath. Tactile sensors register continuously when the skin, muscles, tendons and joints are stretched, contracted, pressurised, turned, shifted and put under strain. Observations have shown that it is vital for many newborn mammals to be licked over their whole body by their mother. If this does not occur for whatever reason, (especially in the abdominal region), the newborn often dies of a functional failure of the urogenital system and/or the digestive system. Hand manipulations and bodily contact are essential requirements for many animals and almost every animal and human being enjoys being stroked or having their skin stimulated in a pleasant way. Animals begin intuitively to bite or rub themselves in any painful area, and we humans also intuitively rub any area where we have knocked ourselves, in order to lessen the pain. This is basically the primordial form of massage!

Preliminary Exercise 2:
Perception with the tip of the finger

Place the tip of an index finger onto a rough surface and keep it lying there very calmly. After a minute at the most, the sensory cells in connection with the touch are unable to perceive what the condition of the surface is. In fact, you will hardly be able to sense that you are touching something. If you now move the fingertip, other sensory cells are stimulated, so that you are able to sense the surface of the object again for a short period of time.

Massage is implemented in animals and humans if their locomotive system shows discomfort, in order to relax, warm up and stretch muscles and tendons, and in this context they have a more mechanical character. In addition, massage performed in accordance with Chinese medicine also works energetically and causes the vital Qi energy to flow. A lack of energy means that the supply systems – blood circulation, lymphatic system and nervous system – perform insufficiently and the anatomical structures that are connected to the supply systems, such as muscles, tendons, joints and the skeleton, are insufficiently supplied.

Preliminary Exercise 3:
Human guinea pig

Ask one of your friends if you may practise the hand manipulations on them. The human test subject is able to give you feedback as to how the techniques feel and what you should improve. If you change roles, you can feel yourself how the hand manipulations feel. Try out different pressure levels and find out what is still pleasant or what has become unpleasant. Once you have experienced yourself how a badly executed massage feels, you will be able to understand your horse better.

Your horse should relax completely during the massage. Otherwise, you cannot guarantee that the massage develops its full effect and that the vital energy will flow unimpeded. You will, no doubt, get some feedback if you are doing something wrong. Observe it carefully – then nothing should go wrong. If you practise on another human, you get the feeling for the hand manipulations and will be able to determine the reactions of your horse correctly. If the veteran is standing relaxed, closes its eyes, starts to snort in satisfaction or even yawns, everything is working. If the horse expresses its discomfort by stepping away, laying its ears back or, in the worst case, nipping its handler, you will need to change the massage treatment.

If a horse generally does not like being touched, a vet or an alternative therapist should investigate the causes for this. Often this points to problems, which can lie either in the physical region (pain or unpleasantness, for example, in the muscles, tendons, ligaments, fascia, joints, bones or organs) or in the mental domain (fear resulting from former experiences or the current environment).

Observe the following when carrying out the massage:

- → Remove bracelets, rings or watches before the treatment in order not to injure yourself or the horse.
- → Carry out the massage in a calm environment: if the masseur/se is stressed and cranky, the horse will not relax.
- → Rub the hands together and shake them well before the start of the massage so that they become warm and no harm occurs through the unfamiliar stress.
- → Make sure you keep an upright posture and breathe regularly.
- → Follow the movement of the hands flexibly with the entire body.
- → Implement the hand movement in such a way that they adapt gently to the body contours of the horse.
- → Always keep constant contact with the horse with at least one hand. If you remove both hands in order to place them on another area a few seconds later, this leads to an unpleasant feeling that disturbs the relaxation.

Effects of massage

- improved oxygen supply to the tissues
- stimulation of the metabolism
- increase in skin temperature
- improvement in the muscular circulation
- alleviation of pain
- strengthening of weak musculature
- stimulation of nerves
- increase in the general feeling of well-being
- regulation of the cardiovascular system
- conveyance of a new somataesthesia (awareness of the body)
- strengthening of the relationship between horse and human being.

It is worth the trouble, in any case, to try out the massage as a supportive measure in older horses that have problems with the bi-annual change of coat. Of course, there are some horses that not even physiotherapy can help – in particular if the delayed change of the coat is due not to age-dependent inactivity of the thyroid gland but to Cushing's syndrome (see page 22)

The hand manipulations that are introduced below are developed especially for older horses. They are primarily designed to support the metabolism and have a pain-relieving effect. Find out those techniques that feel good for yourself and for your horse. You don't have to carry out all hand manipulations every time, in particular if your veteran does not want it. If you want to do more, first check with your animal therapist which techniques are suitable for your horse.

In a few cases it is not recommended to carry out a massage – it could cause pain or lead to other harm. The general rule is that areas that are painful should not be massaged. If you have any doubts, have a talk with your vet!

Generally you should not massage in the case of:

- → local inflammation of the skin or other acute inflammation
- → feverish conditions
- → fungal diseases
- → acute injuries (skin lesions, incised wounds, contusions)
- → haematomas, for example caused by a kick from another horse; in this case ossification can occur in the musculature.

Hand strokes

Owing to their effect, strokes are always carried out at the beginning of a massage. In addition, they are introduced during all hand manipulations after approximately 20 to 30 seconds and are carried out after every hand manipulation as a transition to the next, new hand manipulation.

It is almost impossible to do anything wrong by stroking, you can even stroke the horse over its bones.

The effects of hand strokes are:

- improved circulation in the skin
- dilation of the vessels
- warming of the treated structures
- calming the horse
- decongestion of the venous and the lymphatic systems.

Hand strokes are sweeping movements, which are carried out with the entire surface of the hand. You can use one hand and place the other on a part of the horse, or work simultaneously with both hands. What is important is that the movements are carried out rhythmically and calmly. Start with little pressure to begin with, and then carefully increase it.

In order to find the correct pressure, imagine that a thick, slow-flowing fluid, for example oil, lies under the horse's skin, and you want to remove it by stroking. The massage then has to be carried out continuously, slowly and with the same pressure. The pressure should not come from the wrists, but rather by leaning your body slightly against the horse and letting the body produce the pressure. This is extremely important, as the wrists will otherwise soon be overstrained. Begin at the neck and work your way to the back systematically, making sure that the strokes always follow the lie of the hair of the horse's coat.

If the horse has weakly developed physical senses and therefore often bumps against and

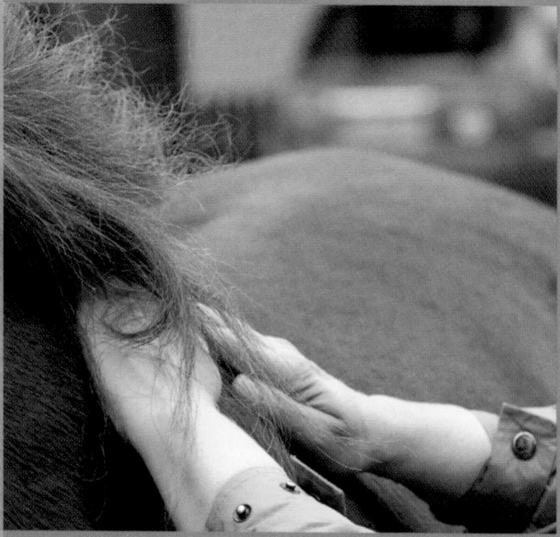

Start with strokes on the neck …

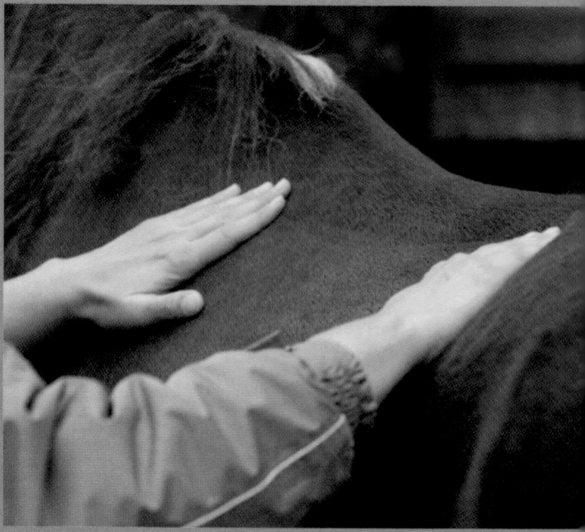

… then stroke over the back …

… and finally over the entire croup.

If your horse is standing in the way illustrated in this photo, or even yawns, you have done everything correctly. (Photos: Beck)

into things, you should carry out long strokes, starting at the ears or even better the muzzle area, and ending at the top of the dock (tailhead). Long and slow strokes restore the 'connection' between the hindquarters and the brain.

Notes for hand strokes

Hand strokes for relaxation are always carried out calmly and rhythmically. Fast movements do not have a relaxing but instead a stimulating effect.

Each horse finds a different pressure pleasant – what one horse enjoys feels ticklish for another. Vary the pressure strength until the horse is standing in a relaxed manner and closes its eyes. Depending on the type of horse, this may require a bit of patience and practice.

Do not apply the pressure from the wrists, but instead use your bodyweight.

Rubbing technique

Rubbing is another form of therapy. Before carrying out the movement, the tissue that is to be treated should be warmed up by means of hand strokes or a thermal roll (see page 87). Hand strokes are carried out (approximately every 20 seconds) during the rubbing manoeuvre and to end the massage (in the latter case in the direction of the heart). This way, they have a decongesting as well as a purifying effect and transport the substances that were released with the rubbing technique into the lymphatic system where they are broken down. You can try out the effect of this massage manoeuvre on yourself, by rubbing the area of the kidneys. The entire area will feel warm and very pleasant. Anybody who performs Qi Gong on himself/herself will be acquainted with this exercise.

Rubbing has the effect of:

- improving blood circulation in the musculature
- stimulation of the removal of metabolic products
- dissolution of adhesions in individual muscle fibres and of scar tissue.

In order to carry out the rubbing technique, make a loose fist. The rubbing is carried out with the straight surfaces of the second (middle) phalanges of the fingers.

The rubbing technique is particularly suitable for the entire top line. Start at the crest of the mane and work your way over the back to

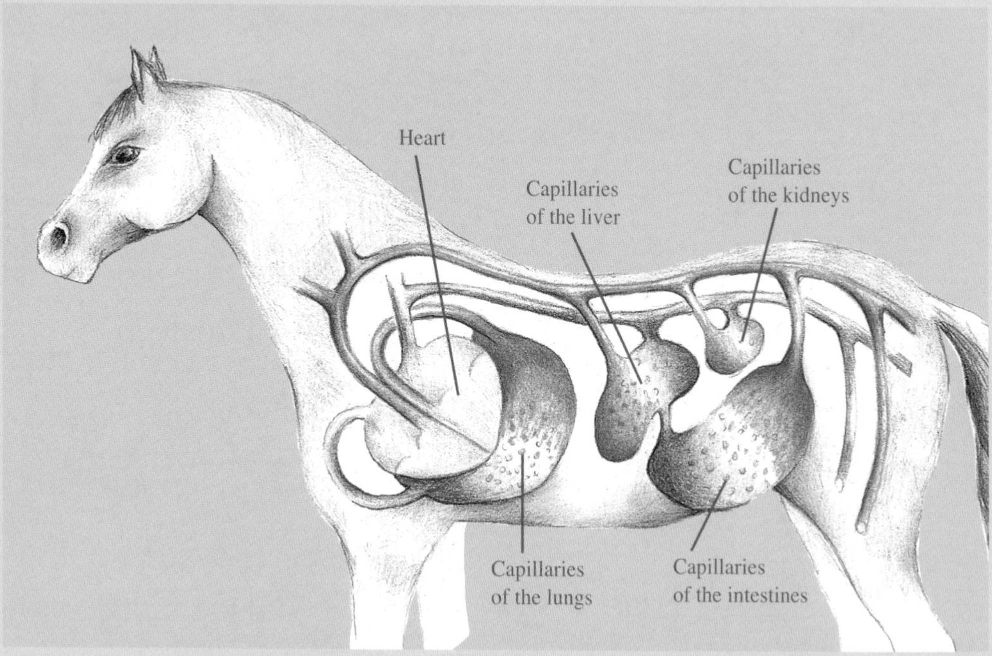

Schematic description of the blood circulation systems of the horse: hand strokes, which are carried out at the end of each hand manipulation and at the end of the entire massage, are carried out in the direction of the heart. This gives them a purifying as well as a decongesting effect. (Drawing: Denmann)

Rubbing can be carried out after the hand strokes on the neck …

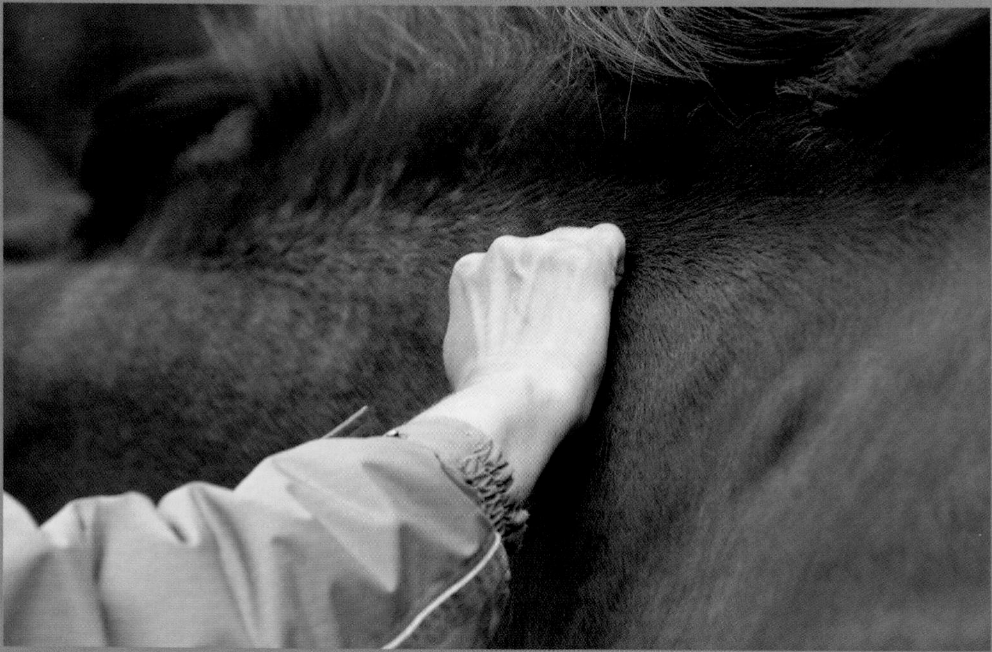

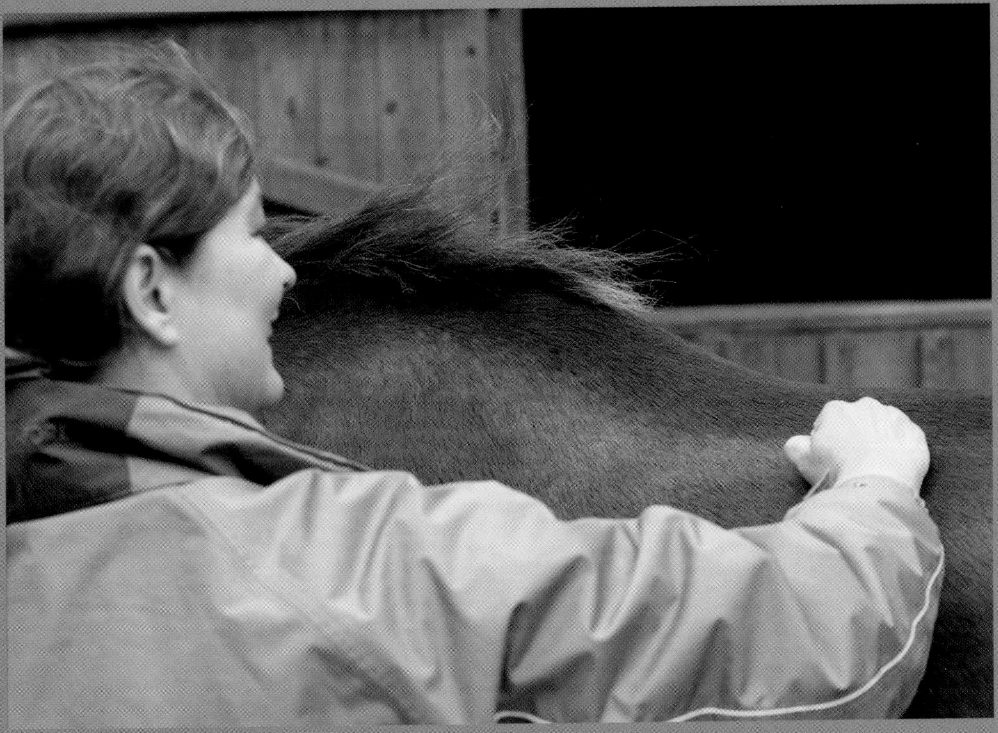

… on the back …

… and on the entire croup. (Photos: Becker)

the croup. The rubbing motion is carried out cross-wise to the fibres, in other words from the top to the bottom on the crest and along the back line. Rub rapidly backwards and forwards – if you are doing it correctly, a strong friction heat is created. It is important never to rub with the joints of the fingers.

Notes on rubbing technique

Never carry out the rubbing motion on the bones or the backbone. Never use the joints of the fingers, but always the entire middle phalanges.

Tapping with hollow hands

Tapping with hollow hands causes a hollow noise. Thus, you need to be careful when using it on horses that have no experience of this massage therapy. They may be a bit sceptical to begin with. Don't start the tapping on the top of the neck in close proximity to the ears when you carry out the procedure for the first time, but rather on the back line. Here, as always, stroking is carried out every 20 seconds and at the end of the hand manipulations.

Tapping with hollow hands has the following effects if carried out gently:

- relaxation of the horse
- loosening up of the musculature

... and if carried out with a little more strength:

- increased blood flow to the skin and the underlying tissue layers
- strengthening of the musculature.

To carry out hollow hand tapping, the palms of the hands are curved slightly inwards, as if you were scooping up water. This forms a hollow cavity in the palm of the hand.

Tap the top line of the horse to the right and the left of the backbone, in other words the crest of the mane, the back line and the croup, with the hands in this position. Never tap on the backbone itself.

The palm of the hand is curved slightly inwards as if you were scooping up water. (Photo: Becker)

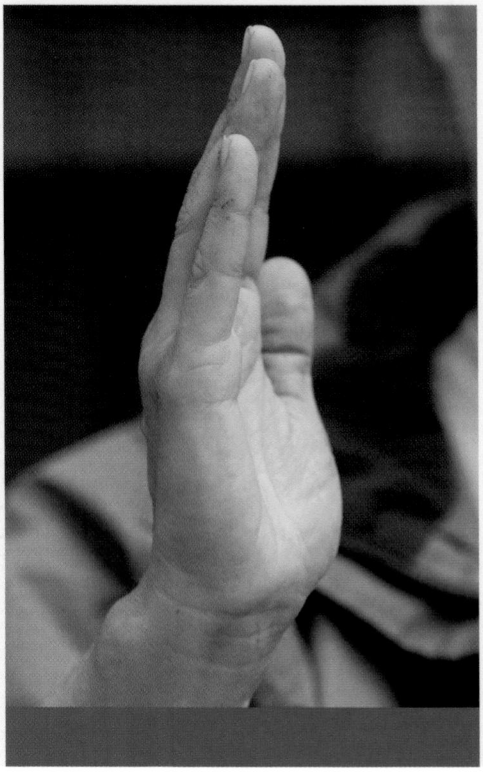

Hollow hand tapping …

… on the neck …

… on the back …

... and along the croup with small, fast movements ...

... ensure a feeling of well-being and assist blood flow. (Photos: Becker)

Notes for hollow hand tapping

Never tap on the spine.

Be careful with horses that are sensitive to sound.

Circling the joints

On cold and rainy days in particular, you will have to care for the restrictions of movement in the joints. You cannot cure arthrosis however; you can at least alleviate the pain with purposeful hand manipulations.

Do not put any pressure on the joints and bone prominences, they are only circled rhythmically and very carefully with the entire hand. As a practice beforehand, circle your own knee with your hand. You will see how pleasantly warm the area becomes. Once you have found a rhythm which is pleasant for yourself, try out these hand manoeuvres on the intercarpal, pastern and hock joints of your horse.

The important measure when carrying out this massage is to make sure that you are safe! Find the safest position for you and don't let your eyes stray from the horse for a moment. If the veteran is nervous and restless, you should not squat next to a leg but rather work in the safety zone, even if this means that the massage may possibly not be as good. Another option is to stop the treatment temporarily.

Circling the joints has the following effects:

- improved blood flow
- alleviation of pain
- stimulation of the synovial fluid.

Start on the limbs near to the abdomen, work towards the hooves, and always end the hand motion in the direction of the abdomen.

Both hands hold the joint, closely enclosing it, and circle the joint without pressure from the bottom upwards. The movement from the bottom upwards is important so that the lymph is not congested at the bottom of the leg causing an 'elephant's leg'. Every now and then, use the hands to smooth out the entire leg from the bottom to the top without applying any pressure.

Notes for circling the joints

Make sure that you are safe! Dispense with squatting next to the leg if your horse is very restless, easily startled or nervous.

Never work on the joints with pressure.

Start the process at the top of the limb and work your way down to the hoof, smoothing out the limb at intervals, always in the direction of the abdomen.

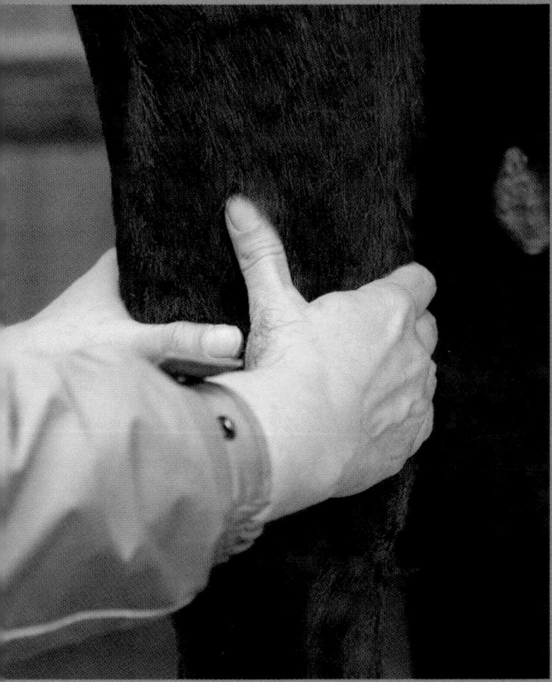

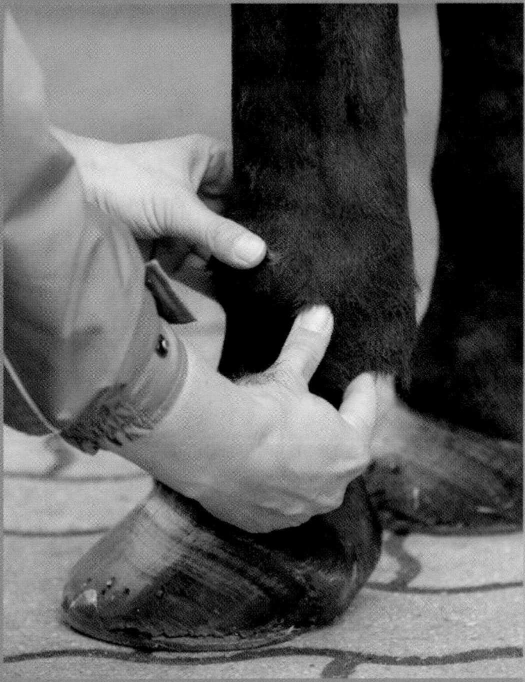

Circling the intercarpal joint.

Circling the pastern joints on the front leg.

The massage of the hind legs is carried out starting from the abdomen and working down towards the hooves, always smoothing out the limb at intervals, and always in the direction of the abdomen.

Circling of the hock. (Photos: Becker)

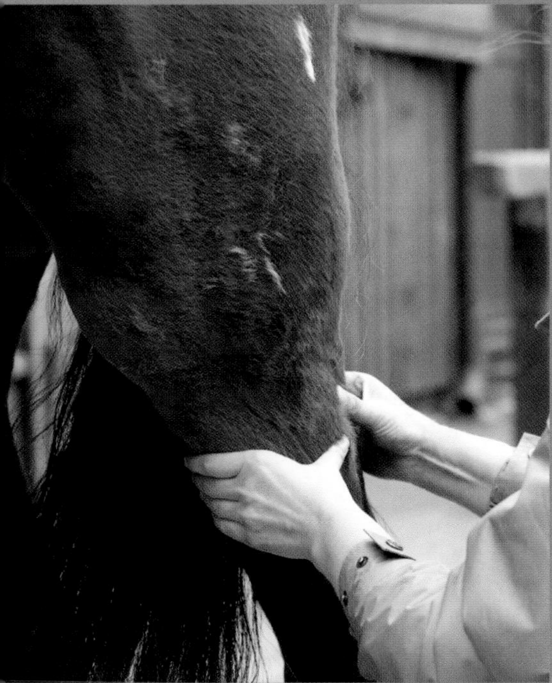

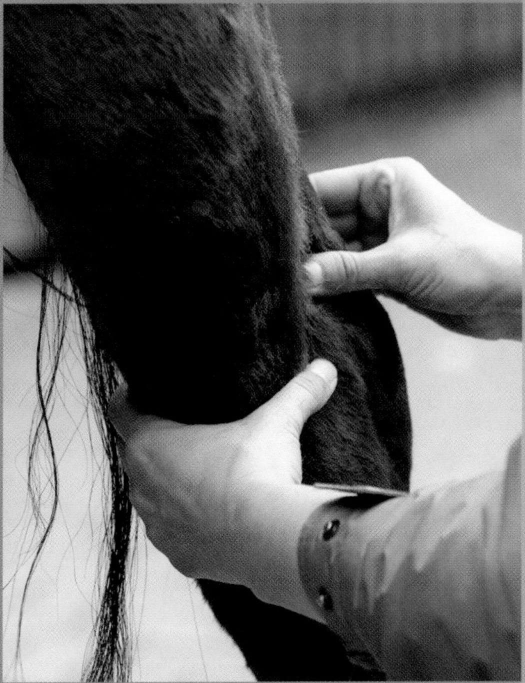

Stroking from the base of the ear to its tip has an enormously relaxing effect on the horse. (Photo: Becker)

Ear massage

The French physician and physicist Dr Paul Nogier discovered in 1951 that there are a multitude of reflex zones in the ear of a human being. He had an intuitive realisation in which he realised that the pinna (ear cartilage) corresponded to an embryo standing on its head. It is assumed that horses also have corresponding connections.

Ear massage, carried out quickly, has the following effects:

- alleviation of pain
- an aid in the case of shock

... and carried out slowly:

- mental balance
- deep relaxation.

Stroking the ears immediately after an accident or before and after an operation supports the stabilisation of the cardiovascular system.

Carefully wrap your hand around the ear of your veteran. The thumb is placed on the inside of the ear, the other fingers on the outside. Imagine you were holding a flower petal between the fingers an thumb, which must not be broken – the strokes have to be carried out with the same care. Now stroke several times from the base of the ear to the tip of the ear, stroking over a different area of the ear every time until you have circled the entire ear. Horses that do not let anyone touch their ears may suffer from blocked cranial sutures ("poll evil"). Such blockages develop, for example, if the horse gets tangled up in its headcollar. Cranio-sacral therapy by a therapist trained in this area can help in this case.

Notes on ear massage

The ears are treated singly, one following the other.

The ears are stroked as carefully as if you had the petal of a flower between your fingers, which must not be broken.

Every square inch of the ear is treated in this way.

If the horse is in a state of shock, the ear massage supports the cardiovascular system.

Claw hands

This manoeuvre is well suited to horses that already have problems with their respiratory system, because the intercostal muscles serve to help the horse breathe in and out. Horses that do not have any problems also often find this manipulation very relaxing. To perform this massage, form the hands into two claws, and pull the fingers along the intercostal space (see photo on page 86).

Claw hands massage has the following effects:

- support of the blood flow to the skin
- support of the blood flow to the intercostal muscles
- loosening of the intercostal musculature in horses that suffer from coughing, and thus an improvement in the horse's breathing.

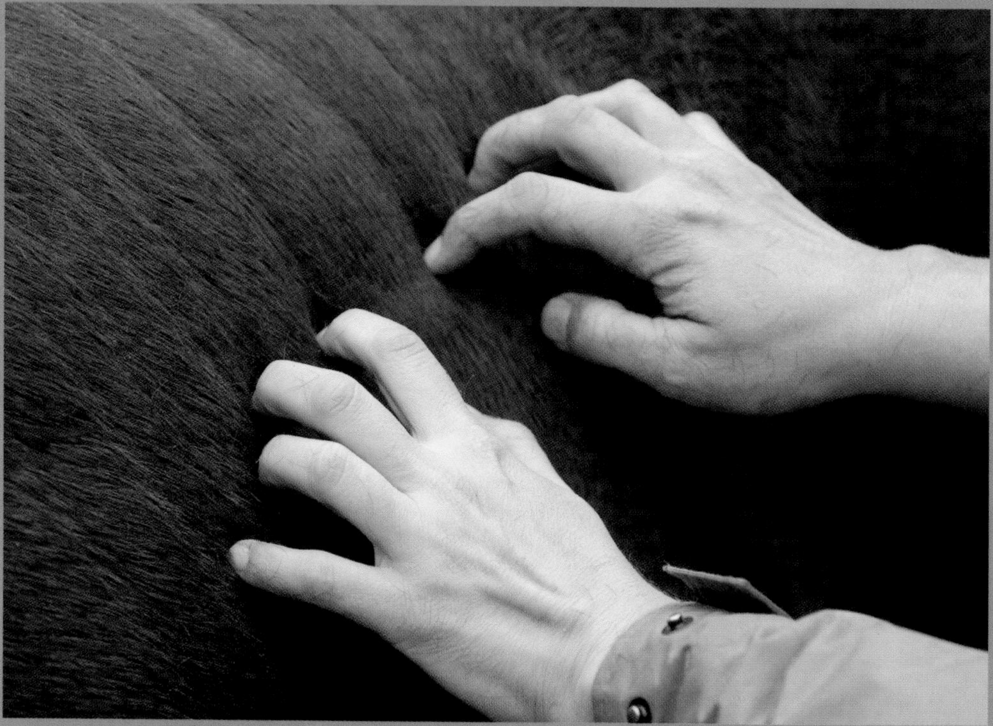

Form a claw with your hands and then stroke the horse, beginning on the back and continuing downwards in the direction of the abdomen.

Most horses enjoy this hand manipulation.

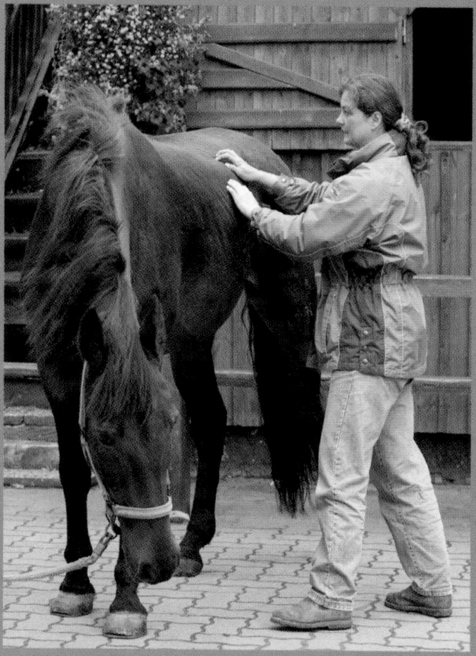

Horses can look this alert after the massage. (Photos: Becker)

Heat treatment is of great benefit

You can help your veteran greatly, especially in wet and cold weather, through the application of heat treatment. Heat has a pain-alleviating effect in arthritic joints and facilitates movement.

The back is also grateful for any thermal treatment, because horses often suffer from tension of the back musculature. The heat supports the blood flow in these muscles and therefore leads to relaxation.

Before performing a massage, heat can work especially well to improve the blood flow of the musculature. Areas that are contracted feel less pain if treated with heat, the veteran is able to accept the massage and relax, and the massage has an even more intensive effect.

Heat has the effect of:

- improving blood flow in the treated area
- relaxation of the musculature and the release of spasmodic states
- alleviation of pain.

Some horses do not like heat. If your older horse reacts negatively to heat treatment, first make sure that the heat source is not too hot. Under no circumstances force the horse to accept the heat if it refuses it for reasons that are not possible to discern – don't apply the treatment. Animals usually know what's best for them.

Notes for heat treatment

Never use heat treatment in the case of acute inflammation (have a word with your vet).

Always make sure that the application of heat does not lead to burns. Tip: always test the temperature on the inside of your underarm, just as you would test the temperature of a baby's bottle. If the heat feels pleasant to you, no burns will occur.

Heat sources

A quick and simple method is the hot-water bottle brought down to a pleasant temperature. Hold the hot-water bottle against the joints. It can also be placed on the back or the area of the flanks and a blanket or rug spread on top to preserve the heat. During the time during which the heat is having its effect, the older horse can be groomed, massaged or fed.

If you want to make more of an effort, a hot roll can be applied. The advantages of the hot roll are that it keeps its heat for a long time and that the dabbing of the hot roll on to the affected areas has a slight massaging effect. It has the effect of an intensive local heat stimulation.

Making a hot roll: fold a standard sized towel once along the longer side.

Roll up the towel in a funnel-like shape.

Then wind a second and if necessary a third towel in a straight line around the first, funnel-like towel. Fill the funnel that develops this way with hot water (45 to a maximum of 70 degrees celsius). Pour in the water with care and hold the roll at a slight angle in order not to burn yourself. Once the temperature of the completed hot roll feels pleasantly warm to touch on your own forearm, you can begin to work on the horse …

… not, however, before first showing the horse the hot roll.

Now the hot roll is placed for a second or two on the area that needs treatment.

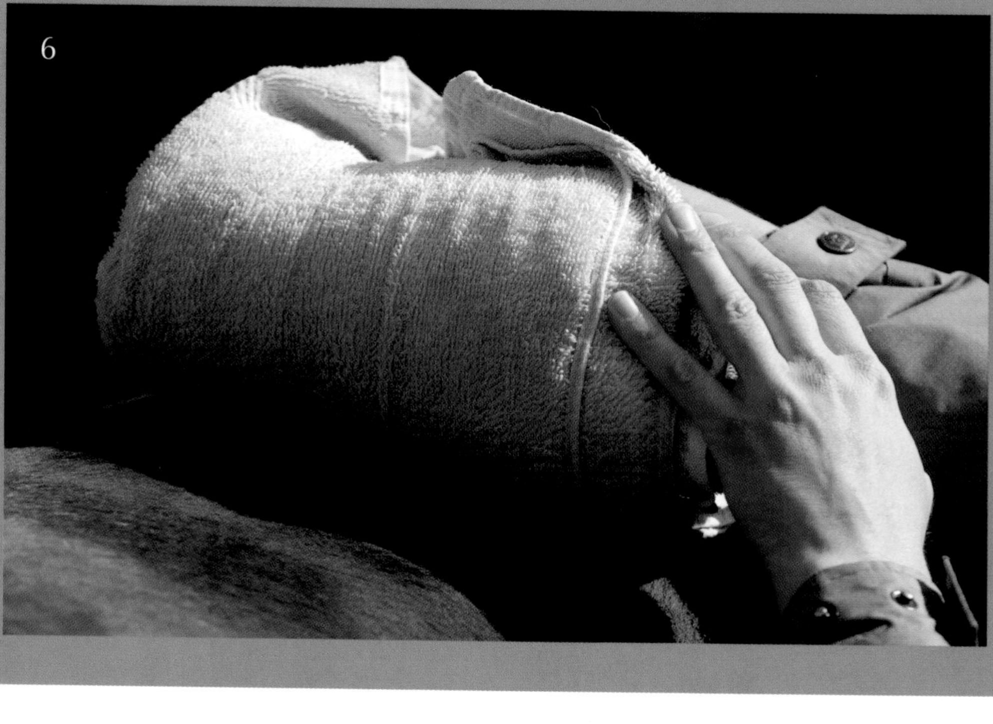

When the outside layer cools off, the towel is unwrapped bit by bit and the inside is still pleasantly warm. In this manner, the treatment can be carried out for up to 20 minutes.

The joints can also be treated successfully with the hot roll. (Photos: Becker)

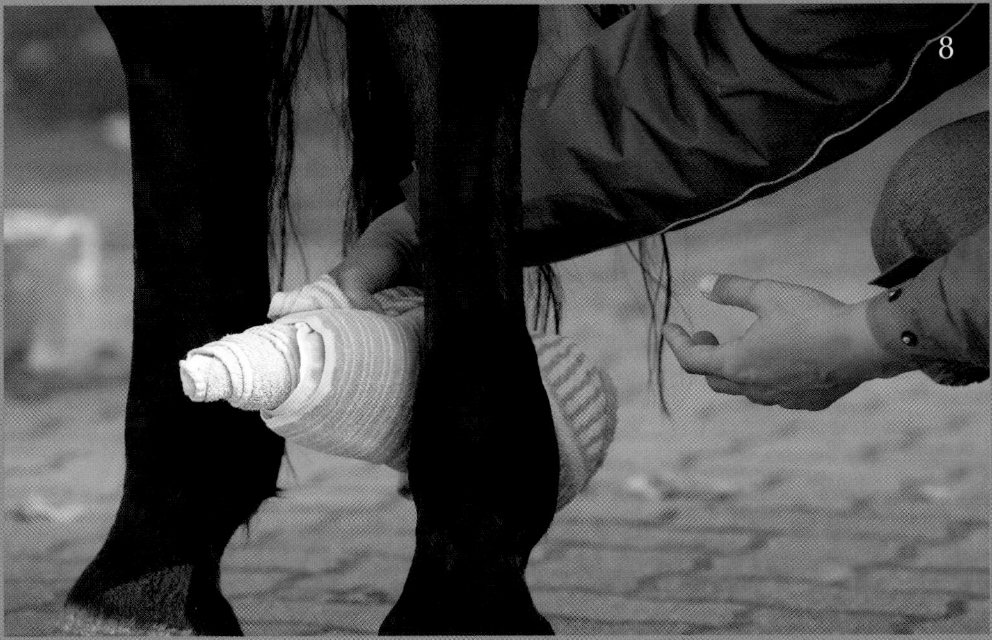

Holistic healing methods

More and more alternative therapists for animals, as well as vets, are offering numerous alternative healing methods for the holistic treatment of the horse. Often they can definitely improve the quality of the life of the older horse. In every case, however, it is important to seek advice from a trained therapist who has proven his/her qualification through successful treatments. It is not advised to self-medicate with little 'pills' – alternative naturopathic medications can have severe side-effects in some cases! In the case of some healing methods, however, it is possible that the owner can apply them to his/her own horse after having been taught how to do so by a qualified expert.

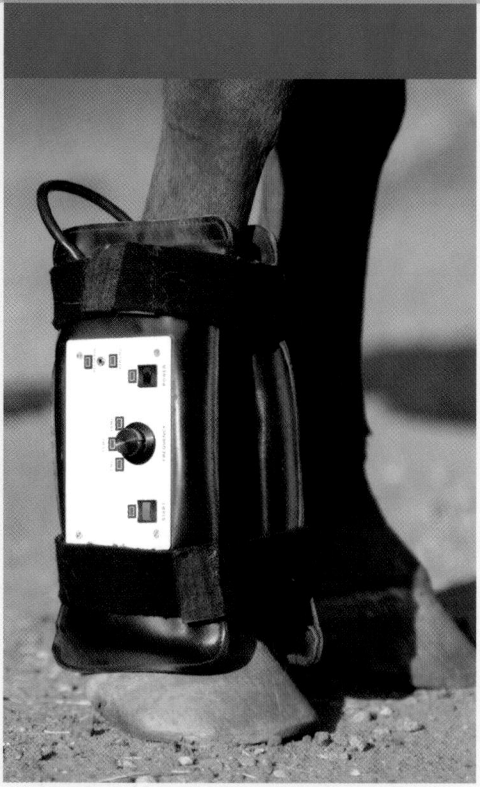

Hand-held units with a pulsating magnetic field, which are run via an accumulator, are easy to apply and can sometimes be hired from the manufacturer. (Photo: Bosse)

Magnetic field therapy

Life on this planet would not be possible without the natural magnetic field of the Earth. Ancient Egypt and the advanced civilisation of Greece already had knowledge regarding the Earth's magnetic fields. In these civilisations people healed with magnetic stones. Today's pulsating magnetic field therapy units are designed in such a way that they have an effect on body cells that are disordered and under-supplied by environmental influences.

The pulsating magnetic field has a positive influence on the psyche, the metabolism, the circulation, celluar regeneration and immune activity.

Magnetic field therapy can be applied very usefully in the case of arthroses, because it improves the blood flow in the affected area, stimulates the regeneration of cartilage, bone and connective tissue cells, alleviates pain, and inhibits inflammatory processes. However, a few treatment sessions are not enough, and you will probably have to delve deep into your pocket to buy one of these rather expensive units. Make sure when buying a unit that you receive extensive advice and will be informed about treatment intervals and the frequency at which you should apply the pulsating magnetic field to your horse in order to achieve the best treatment success.

Finding the effective homeopathic remedy requires an intensive examination and study of the medical history of the horse. Therefore, homeopathy belongs in the hands of vets trained in homeopathy for animals. (Photo: Bosse)

Homeopathy

The founder of classical homeopathy, the doctor, chemist and apothecary Samuel Hahnemann (1755–1843), developed the so-called law of similars. According to this principle, you should use the remedy that would cause the most similar symptoms to those of the ill person in a healthy individual. The homeopath takes time to examine the animal intensively and to take into account the entire history of the horse. Only then can the suitable remedy for the animal be found. Consequently, there is no single homoeopathic remedy for arthrosis or a remedy for problems in changing from winter to summer coat and vice versa. Homeopathic remedies that are not suitable, and incorrectly chosen potencies, can cause significant damage. Therefore, this therapy method should only be carried out by qualified veterinary surgeons trained in homeopathy.

Acupuncture and acupressure

Acupuncture and acupressure are important therapeutic building blocks in traditional Chinese medicine. The term 'acupuncture' is a combination of the Latin words 'acus' (needle) and 'pungere' (puncture). Inserting fine needles into the skin stimulates certain acupuncture points. The aim is to harmonise and balance the flow of the Qi life energy in the body. Acupuncture requires intensive

If the experienced therapist shows you the correct hand manipulations you will be able to carry out acupressure on your own horse yourself. (Photo: Bosse)

training and should only be carried out by a veterinary surgeon trained in acupuncture.

In contrast, acupressure can also be carried out very well by an unqualified person, if he/she asks an acupuncturist to show them the correct technique and the sensitive points. Shiatsu, a gentle treatment method, is also aimed at stimulating the flow of the energy conduction paths, the meridians. There are numerous books to give you instruction. To ensure a successful treatment, however, it is an advantage to study intensively the philosophy of traditional Chinese medicine, which shows distinct differences in some areas from our Western point of view on health and illnesses.

Animal physiotherapy

Physiotherapy is a very old healing method. It has being practised successfully on humans for millennia and is becoming more and more accepted in veterinary medicine. The aim of physiotherapy is the re-establishment, maintenance and support of health in general.

In this context, the animal physiotherapist takes note of:

- → changes in the musculature
- → changes in the other tissues
- → movement restrictions
- → changes in behaviour that point to the existence of pain
- → other signs of pain.

The bandwidth of the physiotherapeutic application is large – the choice of a suitable treatment process is dependent on the individual complaints of the horse. In addition, many therapists have specialised in individual processes. The most commonly used treatments include:

- → massage
- → movement therapy (active and passive techniques)
- → thermal therapy (heat and cryo-stimulation)
- → hydrotherapy (water application; for example, flushing, partial baths, poultices)
- → light therapy (ultraviolet light, laser)
- → electrotherapy (low, medium and high frequencies, magnetic field, ultrasound).

It is worth searching for a well-qualified animal physiotherapist – not just older horses profit from the pain-alleviating treatments, which can significantly increase the well-being and improve mobility. Young healthy horses also profit from it, and regular physiotherapy treatment as a contribution to maintaining health is very much recommended.

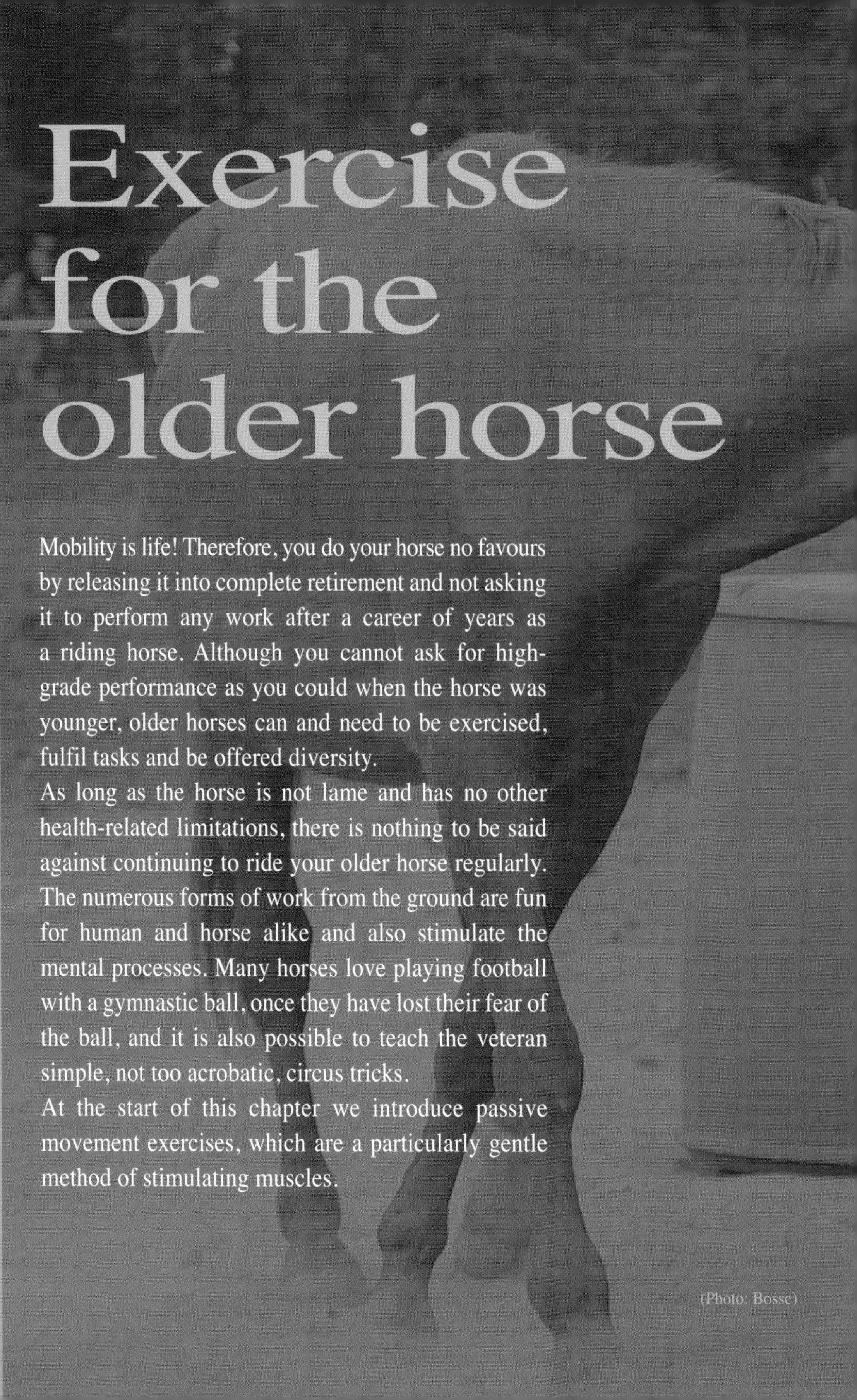

Exercise for the older horse

Mobility is life! Therefore, you do your horse no favours by releasing it into complete retirement and not asking it to perform any work after a career of years as a riding horse. Although you cannot ask for high-grade performance as you could when the horse was younger, older horses can and need to be exercised, fulfil tasks and be offered diversity.

As long as the horse is not lame and has no other health-related limitations, there is nothing to be said against continuing to ride your older horse regularly. The numerous forms of work from the ground are fun for human and horse alike and also stimulate the mental processes. Many horses love playing football with a gymnastic ball, once they have lost their fear of the ball, and it is also possible to teach the veteran simple, not too acrobatic, circus tricks.

At the start of this chapter we introduce passive movement exercises, which are a particularly gentle method of stimulating muscles.

(Photo: Bosse)

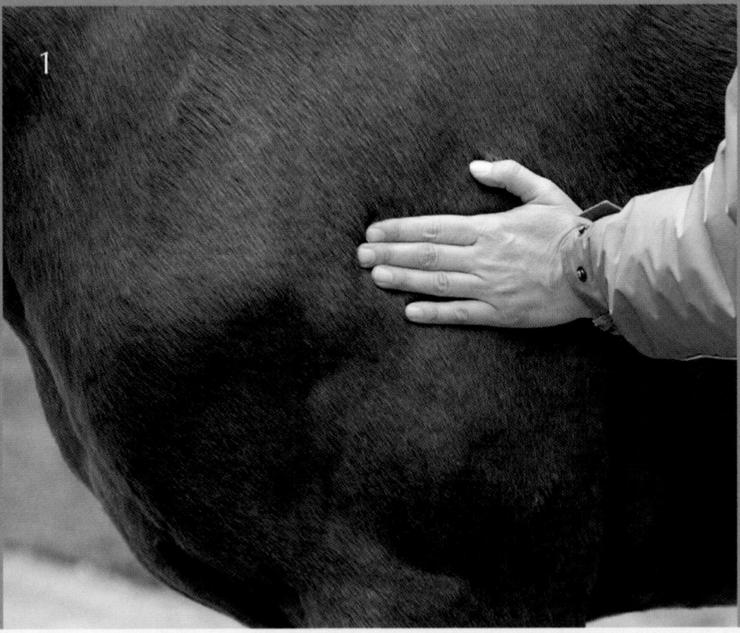

Isometric exercise for the musculature of the forehand: lay the flat palm of your hand on to the upper forearm of the horse in the area of the triceps (three-headed) upper arm muscle (m. triceps brachii) and slowly build up pressure on the limb (1).

Passive mobility exercises

A certain degree of muscle mass can be built up with passive mobility exercises, the so-called isometric exercises, without the animal actually moving. The exercises are suitable for the muscles of the fore and the hind limbs as well as for the muscles of the abdomen and those of the back.

Carrying out these exercises by applying pressure to certain points with the open palms of the hands creates a counter-pressure in the horse. Use just enough pressure for the horse to lean lightly against the palm of the hand, in order to maintain its balance. The pressure of the hand is applied for a few seconds, 10 seconds at a maximum, and then relaxed very slowly, so that the horse does not overbalance. While you are decreasing the strength of the pressure the horse will swing towards you very slightly.

Adapt the strength of the applied pressure individually: if your horse steps sideways away from you, the pressure is distinctly too strong. If your horse does not lean against your hand, the pressure is not strong enough. Repeat the exercises three times a day over a period of one to two weeks. After that, increase the daily exercise to five times. The musculature can be built up through these exercises over a period of up to six weeks. If you want to slow down the decline of the musculature in the older horse, the exercises should be carried out regularly until the end of the horse's life.

Under certain circumstances you will have teach your horse these exercises at first as it learned in its youth to yield to pressure. The horse will have to rethink its reactions to the new demands made on it. Once the veteran has understood what the human is expecting, it will readily enjoy the exercises.

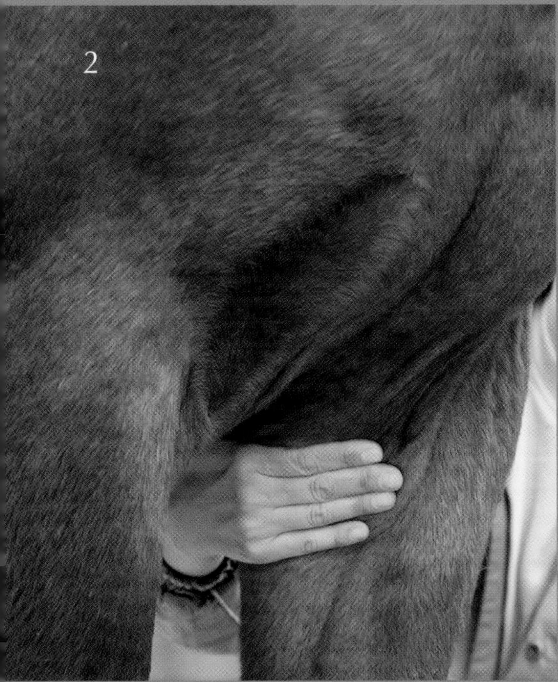

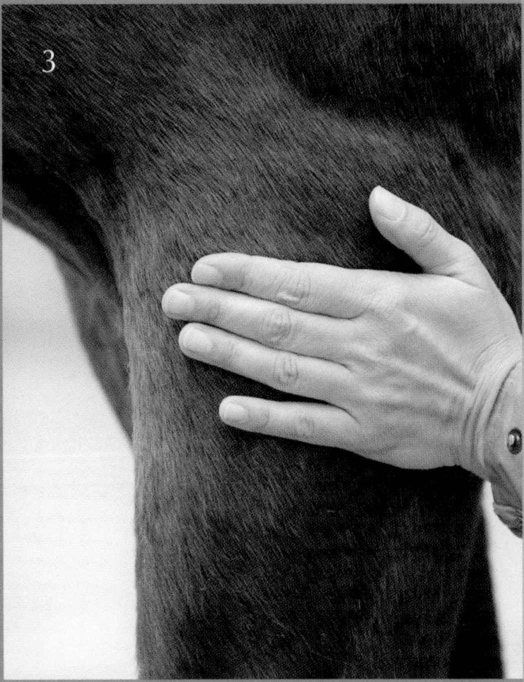

Isometric exercises on the front limbs of the horse: place the flat palm of your hand first from the inside/medial side onto the lower forearm and apply gentle pressure (2). Repeat the same from the outside/lateral side (3), from the front/dorsal side (4) and from the back/palmar side (5). You will find out that it is really not necessary to apply a large amount of pressure on to the limbs, but instead gentle hand pressure.
(Photos: Becker)

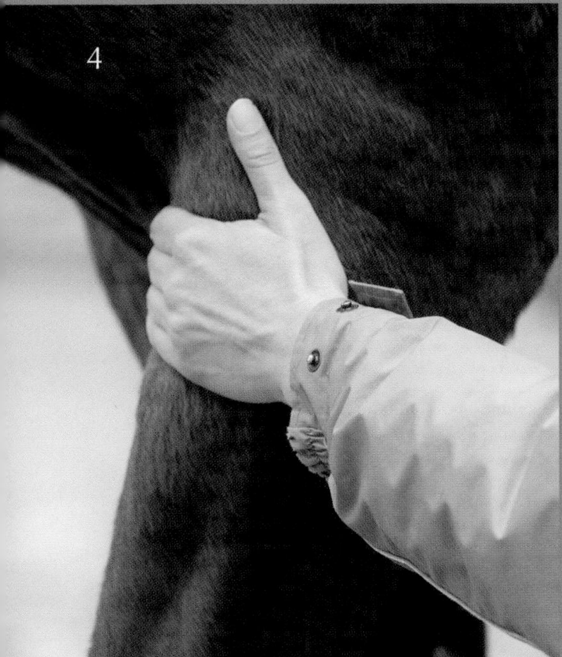

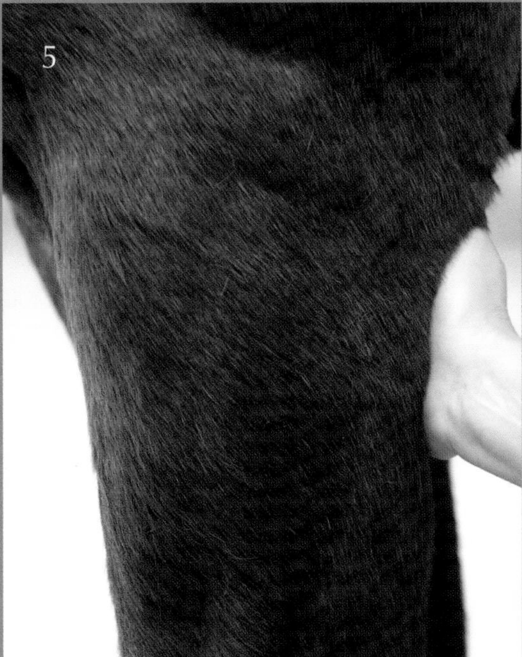

Preliminary exercises for the correct pressure

Place the palms of both hands on top of each other on your chest and apply pressure by pressing the palms of the hands on to each other. You will experience a contraction of your chest muscles. Keep up the pressure for approximately 10 seconds, release the pressure for a short time and repeat the exercise – five to ten times overall.

If you carry out this exercise daily for a number of weeks, the musculature in your chest will begin to strengthen and build up. The exercises introduced here have a similar effect on the horse – apart from the fact that less pressure will be sufficient. You can practise this directly with another person, who presses his hand lightly against your shoulder to the point where you have to apply gentle counter-pressure but are not pushed aside. Hold the pressure for approximately 10 seconds and then slowly relax it. Pay attention to which muscles of your body contract during the application of this exercise – your horse will have a similar feeling when you perform the exercise together.

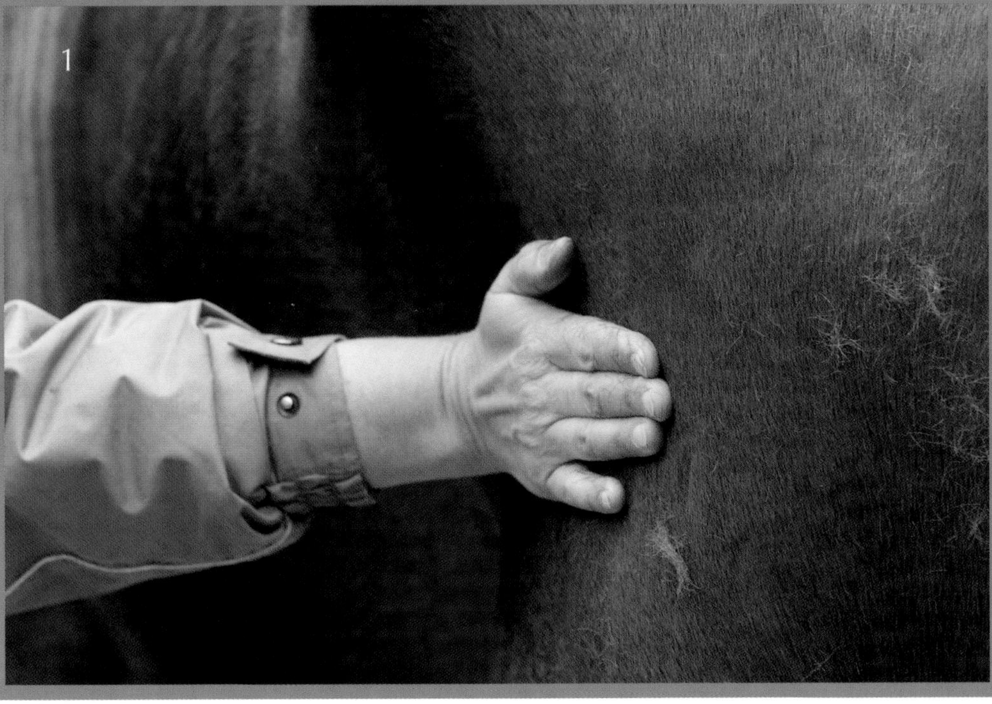

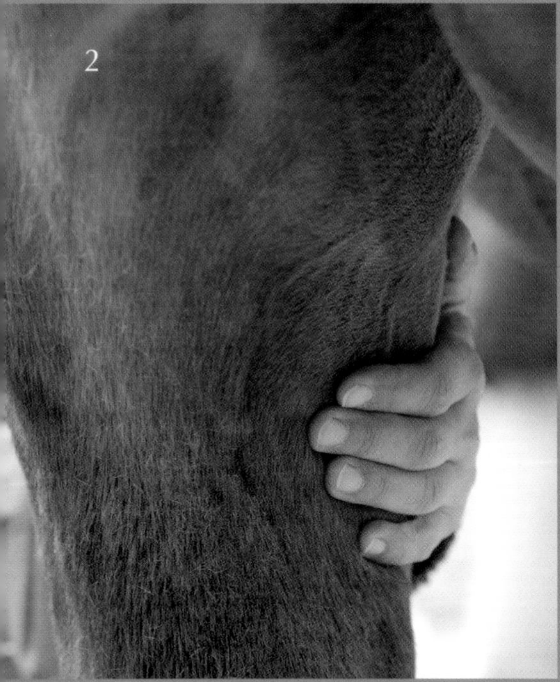

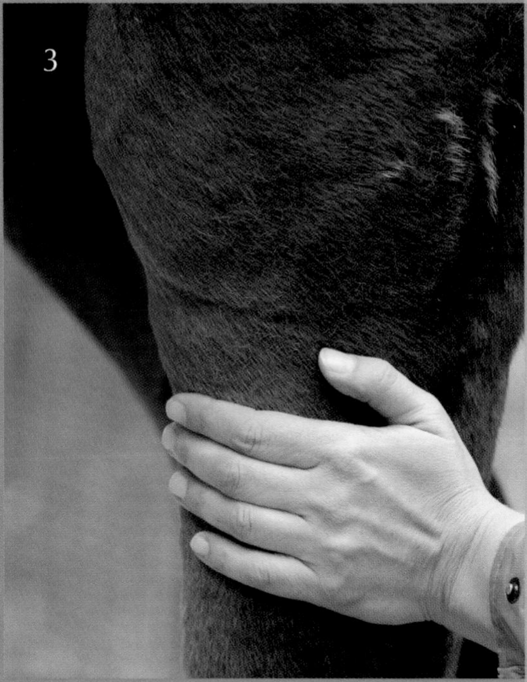

The application of the isometric exercises to the hindquarters is also very effective and stimulating as well as relaxing for the musculature: begin with light pressure from the flat palms of the hand on the horse's thigh in the area of the thigh fascia (Photo 1). Following that, the palm of the hand is placed on the lower part of the limb, from the inside (medial, 2), then from the outside (lateral, 3), from the front (dorsal, 4) and finally from the back (plantar, Photo 5). (Photos: Becker)

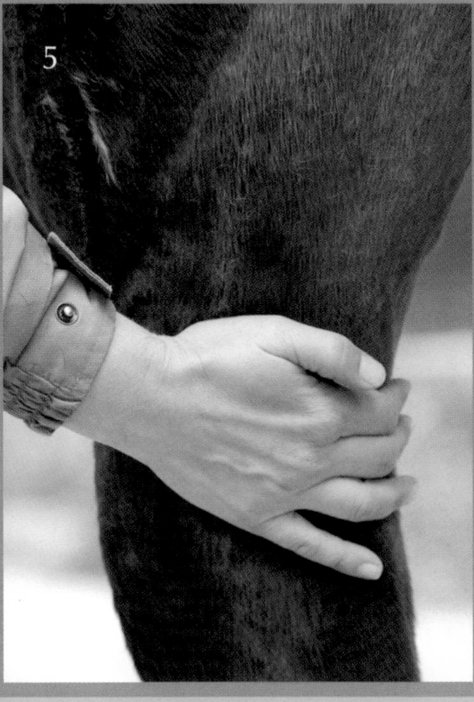

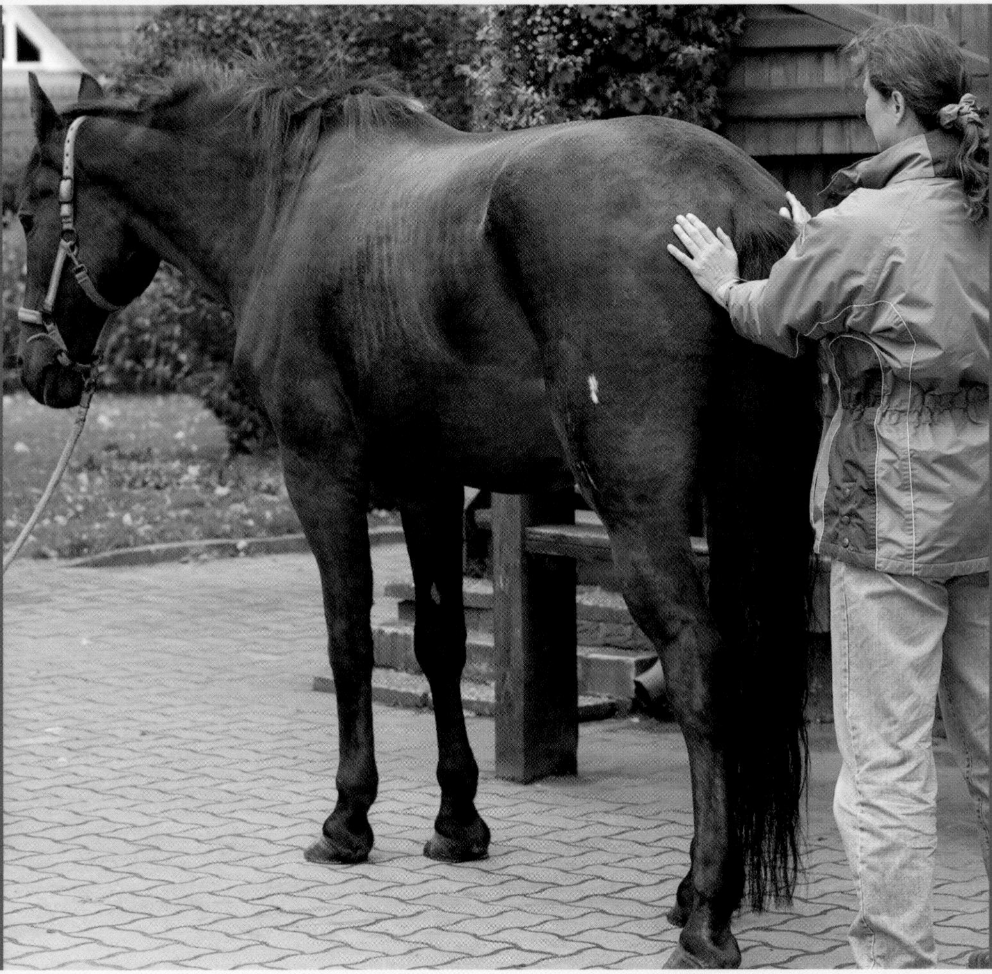

An excellent exercise for the muscles of the abdomen and back: place the palms of your hands slightly beneath the point of the ischium and apply slight pressure with both hands at the same time. Observe how the muscles of the abdomen and the back contract and then – when you remove your hands – relax again. However, do not carry out this exercise if you are afraid that the horse is going to kick out. (Photo: Becker)

Notes for passive movement exercises

Make sure that you are not applying too much pressure – otherwise the horse will step aside constantly.

If you use too little pressure, the horse will not apply any counter-pressure and the exercise is pointless.

Start off with only slight pressure and slowly increase it until you have achieved the desired result.

Active movement

Old people are usually advised that regular exercises and constant training improve the muscle tone and their mobility. Limitations and lack of movement weaken muscles and bones. The same applies for our four-legged veteran.

The state of training of the horse is the determining factor for the reaction time of the sensors (proprioceptors), which transmit the sense of position, movement and strength.

The sense of position conveys the situation and position of the extremities in relation to each other – without requiring visual control. The position of the joints takes a central role in this context. The sense of movement indicates the direction and speed of movement in case of a change in the position of the joints. The muscle strength that needs to be summoned up for the execution of a movement or maintenance of the position of a joint is estimated by the sense of strength.

Proprioception involves amongst other things nerve fibres, the so-called proprioceptors. These include the muscle spindles, the tendon sensors and the joint sensors.

If, for example, the hoof loses its contact with the ground because the horse steps into a hole, the proprioceptors immediately send a message to the brain or the spinal cord and ensure that the horse pulls back its limb as fast as lightning. The better the state of training, the faster the sensors react and the longer it takes for a state of fatigue to occur. In the case of inactivity, these sensors become dormant. For an older horse, this means that the danger of stumbling and injuring itself becomes ever greater, the less it is exercised. Therefore, you need to adapt the training to the physical and mental state of the older horse; also take into account the daily state the horse is in. If the older horse is not well, you should try to find out which exercises it enjoys on such days. If it just wants to be left in peace, respect its wish.

Nothing works without warming-up

It is important that each active exercise is preceded with a warming-up phase of at least 20 minutes, carried out at the walk on primarily straight lines. If the horse is already suffering from arthrosis, the warming-up time should take 30 minutes at the walk.

Trail course

Trail obstacles offer a practically endless diversity of exercises of varying difficulty and they require a lot of imagination and concentration on the part of the human and the horse. Working with poles trains the coordination and physical awareness; the bending and the sideways movements are an outstanding opportunity for the gymnastic training of the older horse.

Trail obstacles that are not too difficult are fun for older horses as well. They support the concentration of the horse as well as its mobility. (Photo: Becker)

Do not forget, however, that as already mentioned the senses of an older horse are beginning to slow down. That means that under certain circumstances you will have to have far more patience with your older horse when you want to teach it new exercises. The important factor in this situation is that not everything has to work perfectly, but instead that the veteran is challenged mentally and that its body is kept flexible and in motion.

An important prerequisite for these exercises is that the horse leads well in hand. If necessary, practise this calmly and without the poles. Always carry out exercises on the trail course with the horse wearing a head collar and a longer lead rope than normal or a lunge rein. Only use a bridle when the horse performs all exercises on the trail obstacles well and you perform them mounted as a further increase in difficulty (as long as the horse can still be ridden).

Before performing each exercise, consider which construction of the course will be the easiest for the horse. If the horse has absorbed this step correctly, do not repeat it then and there, but instead ask the horse to perform it again during the following training session. Once the horse has no problems in performing this step, you can add the next one.

Notes on working with trail obstacles

Make the distances between the poles, barrels, or similar props large enough so that the older horse no longer has to carry out sharp turns.

If the older horse is suffering from restrictions of mobility and has problems moving backwards (rein-back), leave these exercises out of the training plan.

Build up the exercises for the horse logically, step by step. If it cannot understand what you want it to do, it will become anxious or obstinate and the pleasure for human and horse is gone.

Do not develop any ambition, but instead listen to your horse. If it cannot perform some exercises even with the greatest of patience, don't do them. Under certain circumstances, your horse may not be able to carry out the movement you ask it to perform because of illness or disease.

If there are any limitations of mobility in the joints, discuss with your vet which movements should be avoided.

The ground should not be too deep, to protect the tendons, ligaments and joints.

Give your horse the opportunity to take a good long look at the poles before you lead it over the obstacle. (Photo: Becker)

After the horse has stopped with the pole between its front and hindquarters, it is then asked to step forward again. It will have to 'remember' that the hind legs still need to step over the pole. (Photo: Becker)

V-formed poles

Two poles placed at an angle to each other offer many different possibilities. The first step consists of letting the horse step over one of the poles with the front legs, now pause for a moment and then lead your veteran forwards.

Once this succeeds, the difficulty can be increased. For this purpose, in a second step the horse is not led forwards after halting, but is instead asked to step back again over the pole with its front legs (see drawing 1). Drawing 2 demonstrates that you can let the horse step over the first pole with all four legs before asking it to step back.

If the horse is able to step sideways in hand without a pole, you can of course practise this with the V-formed poles, by letting the horse step over the pole with its front legs, halting, stepping sideways two or three strides, before leading it forward and over the second pole (drawing 3). Asking the horse to step sideways the entire length of the pole and only then leading it forwards increases the demands of the exercise (drawing 4).

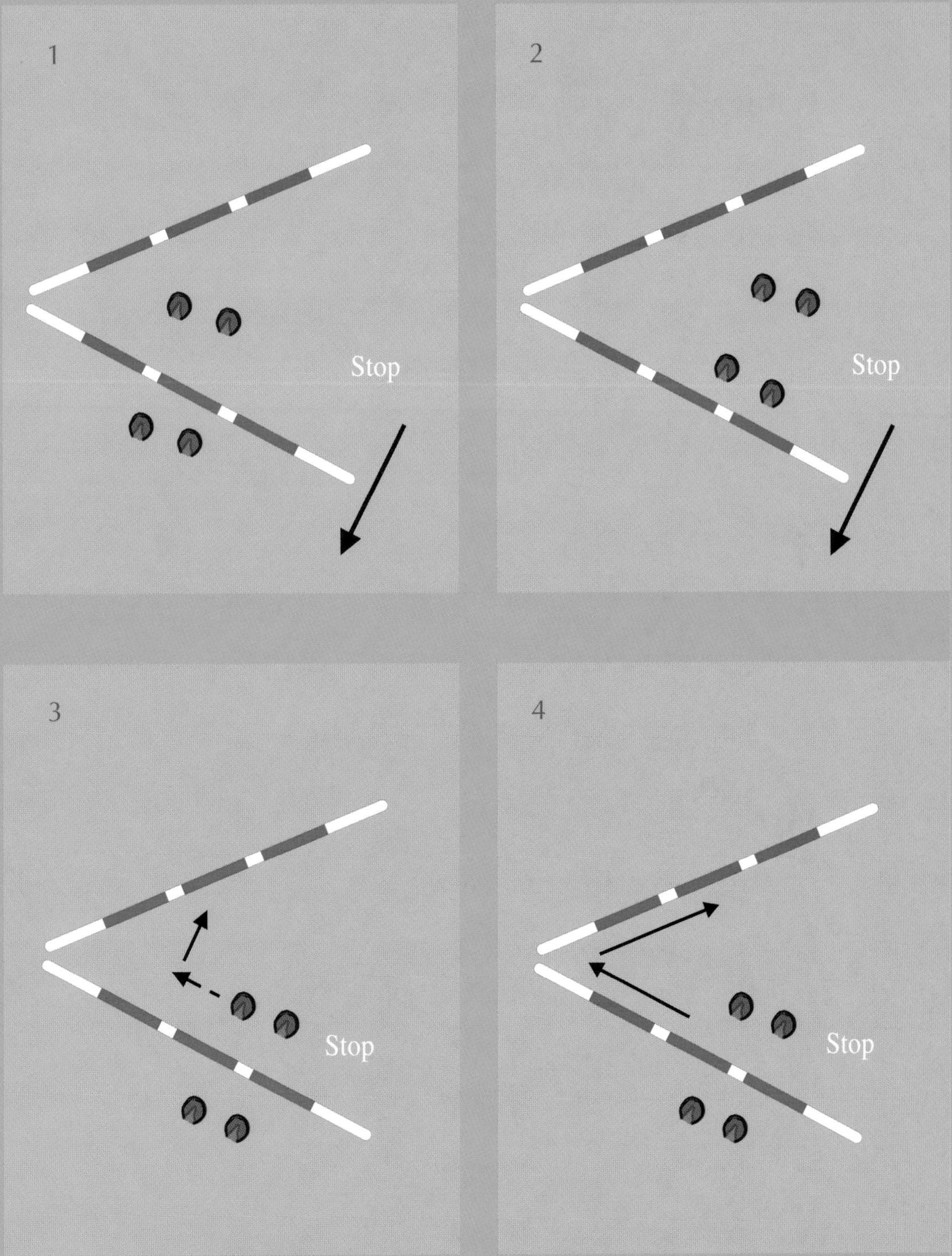
1
Stop
2
Stop
3
Stop
4
Stop

You need four poles to build the U-formed pole obstacle, which offers a diverse number of possible trail exercises. (Photo: Jung)

U-formed poles

You will need four poles to build this trail obstacle, three of which are laid out in U-form, while the fourth pole is placed in the middle, as shown in the drawing.

The first exercise consists of leading the horse through the U, taking care that it does not step over the boundaries. The exercise becomes a bit more difficult if you halt the horse every now and then, in the straight stretches as well as in the bends, and lead it forwards again after a moment's pause.

1. Walk forwards through the U

2. Walk forwards through the U, halting at times (in the bend as well as in the straight stretch).

It is also possible to halt your horse and ask it to rein-back two or three strides in the U-formed poles obstacle. Then lead it forwards again. This is relatively easy in the straight stretches, but it requires quite a bit of coordination between human and horse to rein-back in the bends. Horses that enjoy reining back can be asked first to walk forwards through the entire U-pole obstacle, then halt and finally rein-back through the entire obstacle.

The most demanding exercise in the U-pole obstacle is as follows: lead the horse forwards through the first stretch of the U, then let the horse stride sideways over the second stretch, and finally exit the U-poles by reining back through the third stretch (see drawing below).

Placing six poles so they look like two inverted Us locked into each other, the so-called poles labyrinth, is a further increase in the demands you ask of your horse. As with the U-formed poles, all exercises can be carried out in a more detailed form – just the right thing for trail course professionals!

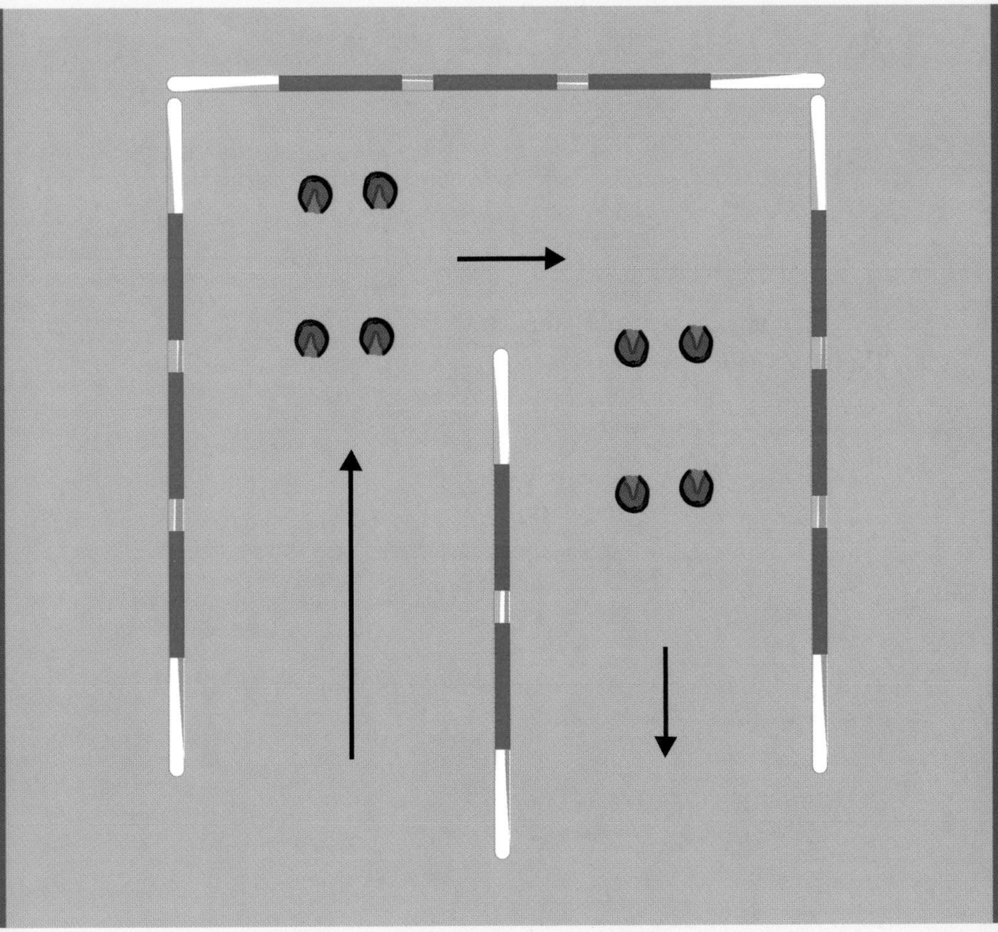

If the horse has not been introduced to the barrels yet, poles are a useful barrier on the sides. For the first exercise, the horse is led straight through the narrow passage between the barrels and poles.
(Photo: Jung)

The barrels

Bending exercises around the barrels have a suppling gymnastic effect on the horse. Reining backwards through the barrels in a serpentine, in particular, trains the awareness of the body. In addition many horses find the barrels very interesting and are familiar with the unusual objects in no time at all.

You will need three or four barrels, which are placed in a row at a sufficient distance to each other. Additionally, you can place poles to the right and to the left as lateral barriers. If you have no barrels available old car tyres or traffic cones piled on top of each other fulfil the same purpose.

If a horse is not familiar with barrels, the first exercise is to lead it straight through the row of barrels and pole barriers. If this works, halt at the end and lead the horse backwards for a stride or two to begin with and backwards along the entire row once the horse is able to carry out this exercise (drawing 1).

The barrels don't come into their own properly, however, until you use them for serpentines. In the beginning you lead the horse forwards through the serpentine, and at the end, the horse walks backwards straight ahead between the row of barrels and poles to the start of the row. At a later date, the horse can also be asked to rein-back in serpentines through the barrels (drawing 2).

1

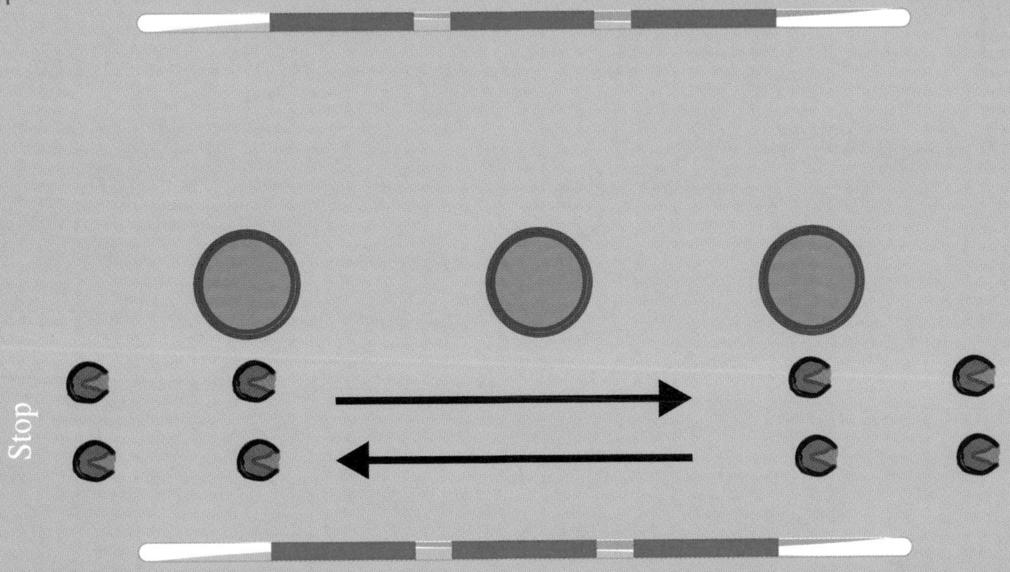

2

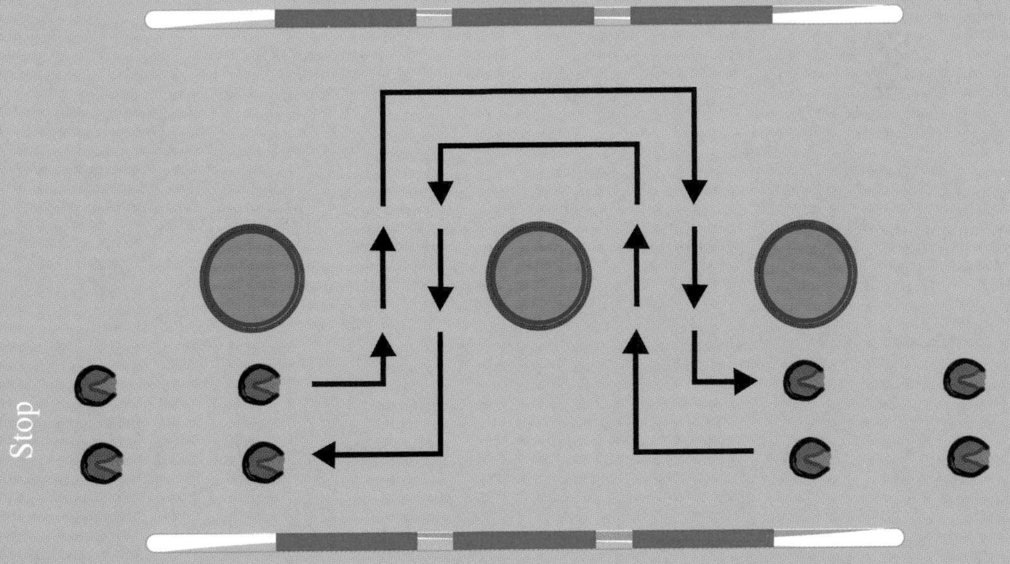

Work from the ground and double lungeing

The older horse can be kept supple and trained gymnastically without being burdened by the rider's weight. In addition, these exercises demand mental alertness. If you use the double lunge correctly, it can relax, stretch and strengthen the back musculature. It is possible to keep the older horse moving well in large circles and straight lines.

It is important to check how much the older horse is still able to perform. If it resists certain exercises vehemently, you should not demand these, as it may well be possible that certain movements cause your horse pain in the joints or that the musculature is no longer strong enough to carry out the movement.

When working from the ground, on the long rein or with the double lunge, the horse should wear a lungeing cavesson or a bridle. All exercises from the trail course (see page 103ff.) can also be performed very well on the long rein, if the horse is used to this kind of work. The changed leading position – you no longer walk next to your horse, but behind it – requires

Horses that were trained from the ground can be exercised and kept fit into very old age with this method. (Photo: Slawik)

increased concentration and dexterity from the human and the horse. In order to avoid faults and prevent dangerous situations – older horses are still capable of kicking out! – the work on the long reins, as well as the work from the ground and with the double lunge should preferably be taught by and carried out under the instructions of an experienced trainer. If the horse and the person handling the double lunge rein are inexperienced, accidents and injuries can occur. You should in every case let somebody show you the buckling-up techniques and use of the lunge rein. A good trainer will work out the exercises with you and your older horse calmly and taking into consideration the performance status of the horse.

Notes on work from the ground

Very important:
Let the older horse walk for at least 15 minutes before beginning with the trotting exercises.

Take into consideration possible pain and the state of the horse from day to day.

Fun and easy exercising of the horse are more important than the personal ambition of the owner.

Bends and circles should be large enough not to put too much strain on the joints.

If necessary, the vet should determine whether the joints are in a healthy enough state to carry out the exercises.

Exercises for the veteran from the ground with bridle or lungeing cavesson:

- Straight ahead at the walk and trot.
- Reining back (not in the case of severe arthrosis in the hocks).
- Walking or trotting forwards straight from the rein-back (strengthening of abdominal and back muscles).
- Stepping sideways at the walk.
- Turns on the forehand and half pirouettes (turns on the hindquarters) at the walk.
- Collection exercises depending on the training and the state of health of the older horse.

Out and about with your older horse

With a bit of imagination, you can design walks with the older horse in such a way that they are interesting and at the same time are training the horse a bit. Use trees on the sides of the road as a serpentine at the walk, branches which are hanging low invite you to walk underneath them, use trees lying on the ground as ground poles.

Even if you cannot ride any longer, going out for walks together with your older horse makes a nice change and intensifies the relationship between human and horse.
(Photo: Slawik)

Include small hillocks, or short, not too steep hills in your stroll at a brisk walk. This supports the musculature of the abdomen, the back and the hindquarters. At the same time you are strengthening your own condition and musculature. Frequent changes of pace cause the older horse to pay attention to you, and not just amble along in the countryside. This includes changes of tempo at the walk, sometimes brisk sometimes slower, or changes from walk to trot and back to walk as well as coming to a halt. To enable the horse to rest in between you can amble along for a while or let your veteran have a few mouthfuls of grass.

Gymnastic for the senior horse under saddle

Many horses are perfectly capable of being ridden even at an advanced age – although the performance capacity decreases bit by bit. However, a lot of older horses seem pleased to be tacked up for a hack, or if they can show that they haven't forgotten by far everything they learned during their past as a dressage horse.

It is essential, especially when riding old horses, to estimate their form on the day. The amount of work can be adapted accordingly, or you may even have to hang the saddle back on its rack unused. If you are riding an older horse you will not be able to circumvent a 20 minute-long intensive warming-up phase, during which it is recommended to lead the horse for a while. A mounting block protects the horse's back – and not just that of an older horse. It ensures that the horse does not have to endure excessive weight on one side, threatening its balance with the effect that the possibly tensed-up back musculature contracts even further.

It should go without saying that an expert checks the fit of the saddle regularly and the saddle is changed if necessary. Especially in older horses, whose musculature is deteriorating a bit, you may find that a saddle which fitted perfectly for years will suddenly fit no longer, cause pressure sores or at least leading to a feeling of unpleasantness in the horse. And maybe you can do without a noseband for your horse, and thus help it breathe more easily.

Simple gymnastic dressage movements help maintain the horse's mobility. In addition, it is important, of course, to take into account how the horse was ridden in the past, in order to determine how to exercise the horse under saddle now. The trail obstacles described earlier are suitable for riding through, as long as the individual elements are not placed too close to each other with the bends therefore becoming too narrow. When you go for a hack, you can use rows of trees for serpentines, branches as poles on the ground or small hillocks for climbing, in the same way as you would when taking the horse for a walk.

Recommended for horses of all ages: a mounting block protects the back of every horse. (Photo: Bosse)

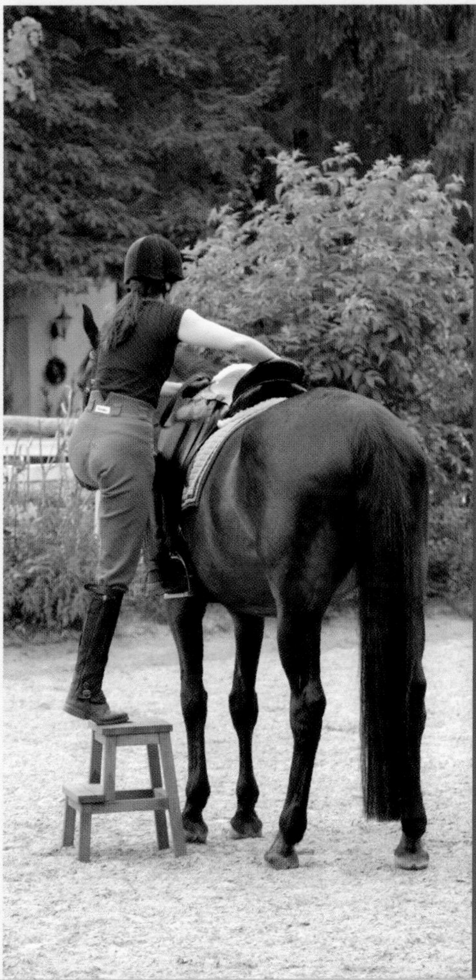

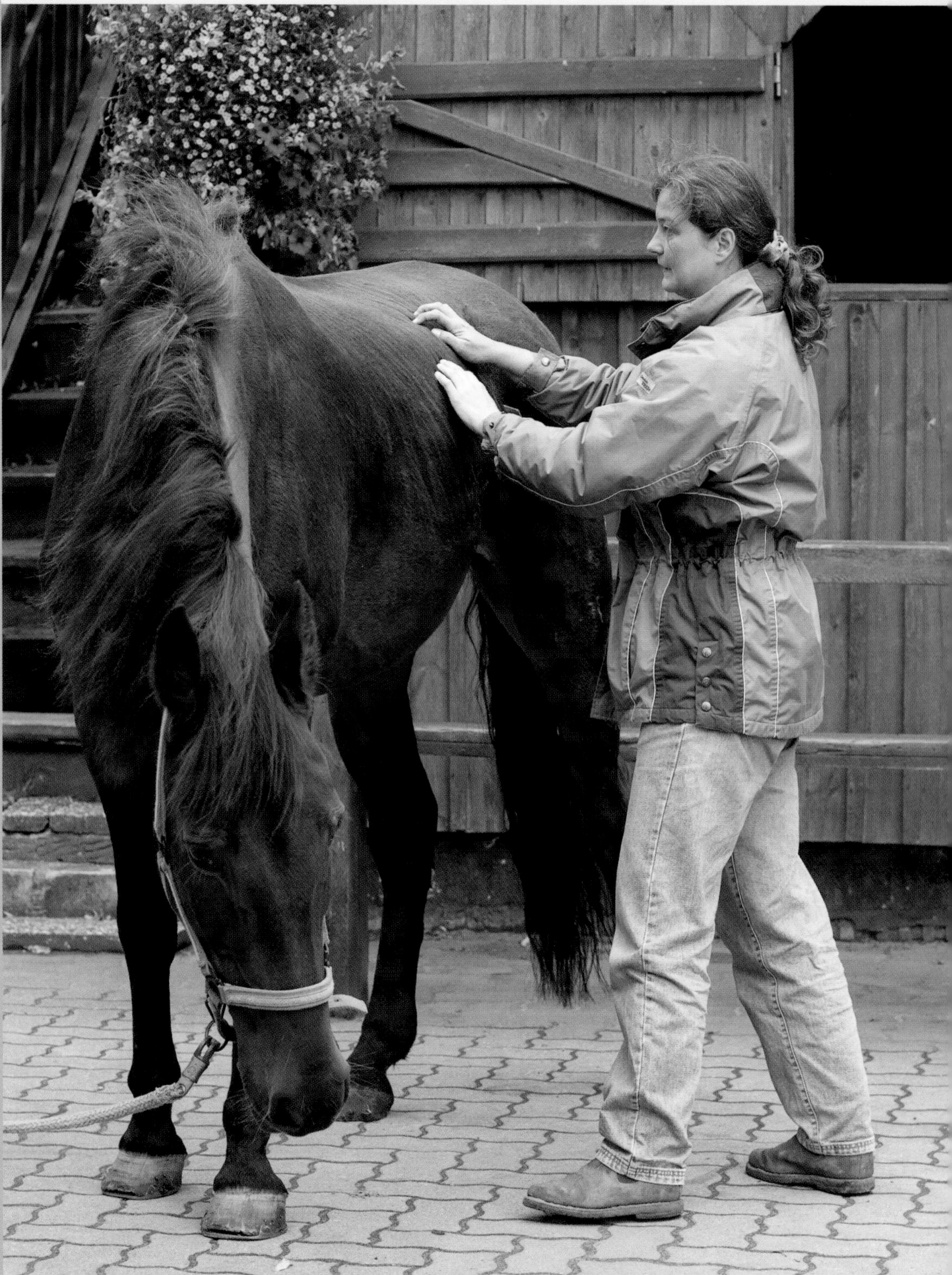

Weekly training plan for older horses

The plan suggested below should only offer a few simple pointers, and should not be understood as a rigid concept. Which exercises you can carry out will vary according to the abilities of your older horse. You should also keep in mind that ageing is a constant process. If, for example, you were able to hack out without the slightest problem half a year ago, your horse may no longer be able to do anything of the sort six months later.

If you do not have time every day, vary the plan accordingly. It is important to offer the horse variety. After all, nobody wants to do the same thing every day.

Monday:	Extensive thermal heat treatment and massage, grooming and stroking
Tuesday:	Thermal heat treatment, approximately ½ hour work from the ground
Wednesday:	Massage and approximately ½ to ¾ hour riding (if that is still possible), afterwards another massage
Thursday:	As Mondays
Friday:	Thermal heat treatment and approximately ½ hour work from the ground, followed by a massage
Saturday:	As Mondays and Thursdays
Sunday:	Go for a walk

Preparing for the end

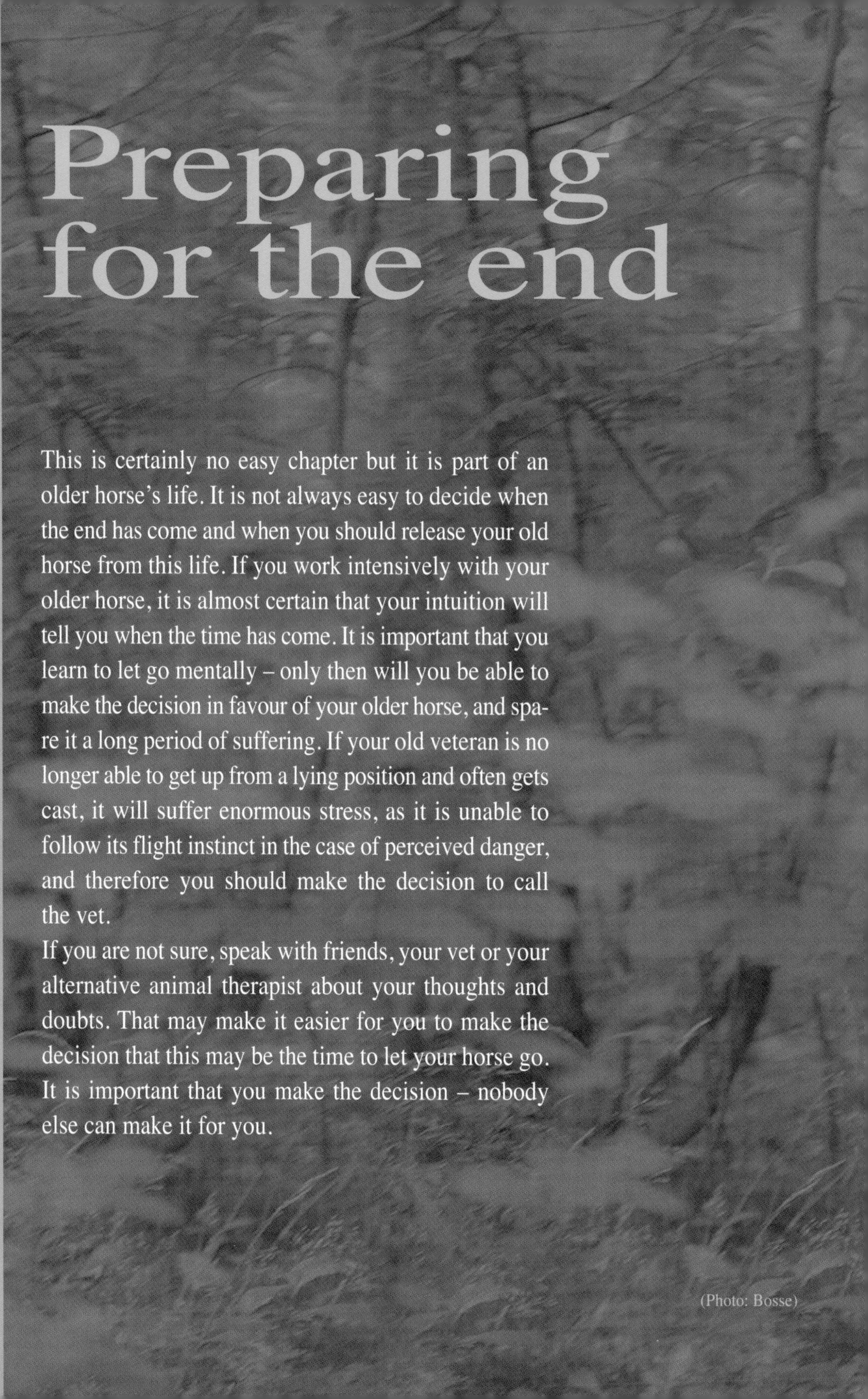

This is certainly no easy chapter but it is part of an older horse's life. It is not always easy to decide when the end has come and when you should release your old horse from this life. If you work intensively with your older horse, it is almost certain that your intuition will tell you when the time has come. It is important that you learn to let go mentally – only then will you be able to make the decision in favour of your older horse, and spare it a long period of suffering. If your old veteran is no longer able to get up from a lying position and often gets cast, it will suffer enormous stress, as it is unable to follow its flight instinct in the case of perceived danger, and therefore you should make the decision to call the vet.

If you are not sure, speak with friends, your vet or your alternative animal therapist about your thoughts and doubts. That may make it easier for you to make the decision that this may be the time to let your horse go. It is important that you make the decision – nobody else can make it for you.

(Photo: Bosse)

There are alternative therapists and veterinary homeopaths who have specialised in accompanying you on that last walk. In that case, at least, you will not have to go it alone. If possible, be there for your horse at the end – irrespective of whether your horse is going to be put to sleep or dies naturally. Bach flower therapists often recommend the Bach flower of the walnut as an aid – this eases the way for the respective animal. On the other hand it is also the flower for a new beginning and helps the soul in external changes of every kind. Thus, this Bach flower is also suitable for you as the human being, in order to cope better mentally with this phase.

I myself experienced with my horse how important it was for him that I was there right to the end. He had cancer, and for a long time things went very well, but then I observed more and more often that he stood alone, away from the herd, and no longer wanted to play. The tumours had metastasised, and their growth could no longer be controlled. I had to make the decision and then call the vet and the knacker to make an appointment. My gelding knew exactly what was going to happen on this day, but he was ready for it. The only thing he demanded was that I did not move from his side, when I did he became very hectic. With me by his side and a vet who understood the procedure of putting an animal to sleep, he died peacefully. It wasn't easy and I will never forget it, but I was glad that I was able to accompany him right up to the end.

Make sure you decide at an early stage which method of euthanasia you are going to choose for your horse, the injection or the bolt gun. Putting down a horse in a field is permitted. The horse is either put down with a bolt gun, or by administering chemical medication into the bloodstream (putting it to sleep) by the vet. The knacker is responsible for the transportation and disposal of the carcass – leave the phone numbers at the livery yard, so that you can act quickly in the case of an emergency.

There are different methods of putting a horse down with medication. Some vets prefer to sedate the animal and then inject the euthanasia medication, other vets give the euthanasia medication immediately without any prior sedation.

Talk through the procedure with a vet you can trust and who knows your horse. If it is carried out correctly, your horse will sink to the ground in seconds and show only slight muscle spasms and possibly two or three deep final breaths, irrespective of which method you choose. Do not put off the decision or the discussions with the vet, as in many cases you will need to act quickly; this applies not only to older horses. If you are certain of the what, who and when, saying farewell to your horse will be easier for yourself as well as for your older horse.

Appendix

Further Reading

Edward Bach and E.J. Wheeler:
Bach Flower Remedies
McGraw-Hill, 1998

Marion Brehmer:
Bach Flower Remedies
Cadmos, 2006

Renate Ettl:
Practical Horse Massage
Cadmos, 2002

Robert Holland:
Understanding the Older Horse
Eclipse Press, 1999

Chris Olson:
A Hot Line to your Horse
Cadmos, 2002

Sarah Pilliner and Joanna Prestwich:
Care of the Older Horse
J.A. Allen & Co Ltd, 1999

Cathy Tindall/Jaki Bell:
Shiatsu for your Horse
Cadmos, 2006

Linda Weritz:
Horse Sense and Horsemanship
Cadmos, 2008

Websites

Deanna's Equine Library – Health Care
www.ramsaybooks.com/link/health/seniors/

Official Website of the British Horse Society (Books)
www.britishhorse.com/acatalog/stable_management_horse_care.html

Association for British Veterinary Acupuncturists (ABVA)
www.abva.co.uk

Britsh Association of Homeopathic Veterinary Surgeons (BAHVS)
www.bahvs.com

Battles, Hayward and Bower (equestrian products):
www.battles.co.uk

Index

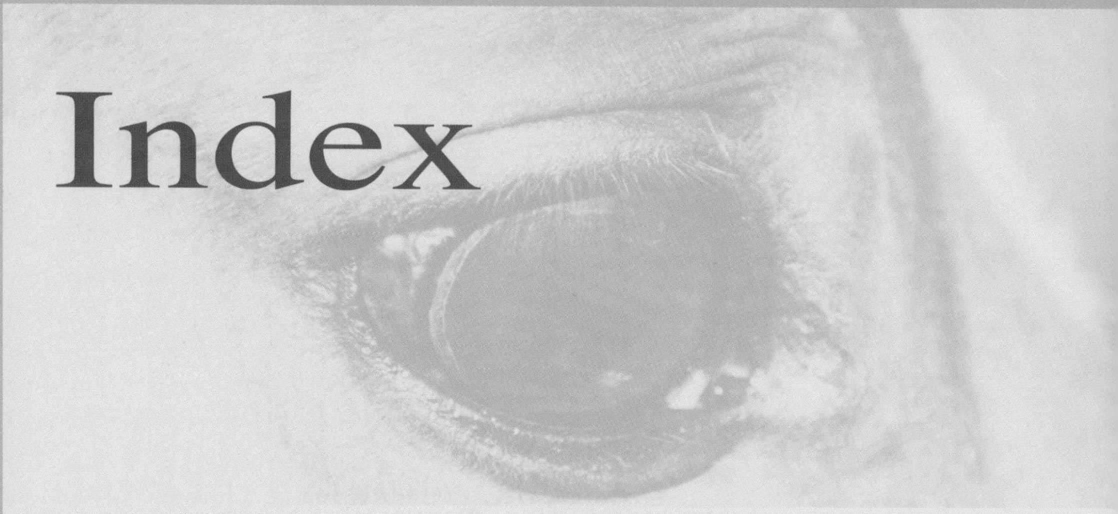

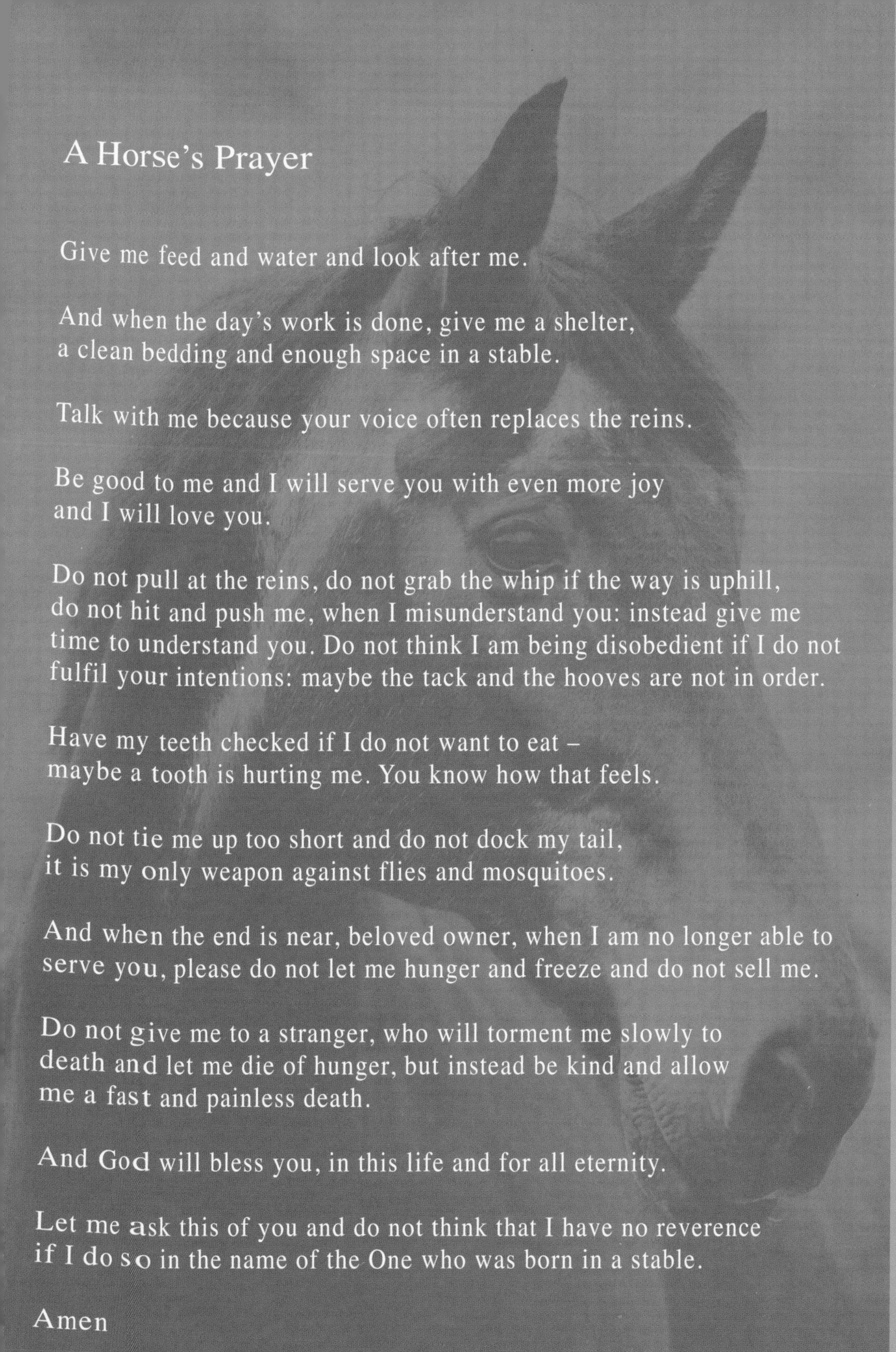

A Horse's Prayer

Give me feed and water and look after me.

And when the day's work is done, give me a shelter,
a clean bedding and enough space in a stable.

Talk with me because your voice often replaces the reins.

Be good to me and I will serve you with even more joy
and I will love you.

Do not pull at the reins, do not grab the whip if the way is uphill,
do not hit and push me, when I misunderstand you: instead give me
time to understand you. Do not think I am being disobedient if I do not
fulfil your intentions: maybe the tack and the hooves are not in order.

Have my teeth checked if I do not want to eat –
maybe a tooth is hurting me. You know how that feels.

Do not tie me up too short and do not dock my tail,
it is my only weapon against flies and mosquitoes.

And when the end is near, beloved owner, when I am no longer able to
serve you, please do not let me hunger and freeze and do not sell me.

Do not give me to a stranger, who will torment me slowly to
death and let me die of hunger, but instead be kind and allow
me a fast and painless death.

And God will bless you, in this life and for all eternity.

Let me ask this of you and do not think that I have no reverence
if I do so in the name of the One who was born in a stable.

Amen

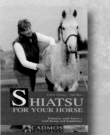